Cooking Up U.S. History

COOKING UP U.S. HISTORY
Recipes and Research to Share with Children

Suzanne I. Barchers
and
Patricia C. Marden

Illustrated by
Leann Mullineaux

1991
TEACHER IDEAS PRESS
A Division of
Libraries Unlimited, Inc.
Englewood, Colorado

TEACHER IDEAS PRESS
A Division of Libraries Unlimited, Inc.
P.O. Box 6633
Englewood, CO 80155-6633
1-800-237-6124

Library of Congress Cataloging-in-Publication Data

Barchers, Suzanne I.
    Cooking up U.S. history : recipes and research to share with
children / Suzanne I. Barchers and Patricia C. Marden ; illustrated
by Leann Mullineaux.
    xiii, 187p. 22x28cm.
    Includes bibliographical references and index.
    ISBN 0-87287-782-5
    1. Cookery, American--Juvenile literature. 2. United States-
-History--Study and teaching (Elementary)   I. Marden, Patricia C.,
1948-   . II. Mullineaux, Leann. III. Title.
TX652.5.B22   1991
641.5973--dc20   90-29867
                                         CIP

Dedicated to Dan, Jeff, and Josh who were always there.
S.I.B.

Dedicated to my family and friends
who all told me not to work too hard and who cared.
P.C.M.

Contents

Introduction

America has a rich heritage of cooking, beginning with the varied diet of the American Indians before the discovery voyages of the Europeans. Cooking in the classroom is an ideal way to enhance the study of American history in the elementary program. Cooking can be an occasional treat or a routine component of instruction. Teachers may use a cooking experience as an integral part of a thematic unit, to culminate a unit, or to observe a holiday. Children benefit from learning basic cooking terms and skills and from the cooperative preparation and consumption of new and different foods.

Cooking Up U.S. History is a compilation of recipes, research, and readings linked to the history of the United States. It not only provides teachers with classroom-tested recipes, but offers them in the context of the most commonly encountered social studies units: the American Indians, the colonists, the Revolutionary War, the westward expansion, the Civil War, and the commonly identified geographic regions of the country. Selected recipes are followed by Library Links that will interest students in further research on the topic. All chapters include bibliographies of related fiction and nonfiction titles for additional study. A separate bibliography devoted to books on food is also included. Helpful information on cooking terminology and measurement is supplied in the appendixes and glossary.

RECIPE SELECTION

Recipes have been carefully researched and selected to reflect the practices of each period. However, since modern appliances, such as mixers and ovens, will be used, the recipes are modernized. Library links may direct students to discover earlier methods of cooking.

The chapter on the colonists also includes recipes for soap, candles, and ink. Though not for consumption, these items are included to illustrate how early settlers had to prepare a variety of necessities.

The number of servings given for each recipe generally indicates normal servings, such as one might have at home. The recipes do provide enough for a tasting party. Many recipes would have to be doubled or tripled to provide enough for a full meal for an entire classroom.

Some recipes accurately reflect the limitations of the food or resources of the time the recipe was written. Therefore, the foods may not be the most tasty or appealing. It is important for these recipes that students understand people often had to "make do." This is part of the adventure of cooking in the classroom!

LIBRARY LINKS

Most recipes include a Library Link that can be used as a research or reference question. The answers to some links can be found simply by consulting a dictionary. Some links are taken from books about food. (See the bibliographies.) Some links require the use of encyclopedias, nonfiction books, or other reference materials. Answers to the Library Links are in appendix A, and they provide fascinating information about the historical period, food, and regions.

INTRODUCTIONS TO THE CHAPTERS

The introductory page to each chapter provides information or an alphabetical listing of terms about the period or region. These ABCs can be used as vocabulary or in trivia challenges.

BIBLIOGRAPHIES

The bibliographies for chapters 1 through 5 (the Indians, colonists, Revolutionary War, westward expansion, and Civil War) are extensive, providing many opportunities for further research or for the use of historical fiction. Bibliographies for the regional chapters do not include titles on specific states or cities. Consult your library for books to supplement your study. There are fewer historical fiction titles in the regional chapters; however, many titles found in chapters 1 through 5 also apply to the study of the regions.

It is difficult to indicate reading levels for these books, as the range of reading ability varies widely in a classroom. If the reading level is indicated as "grades 3 and up," it means that it could be read by the more advanced third grader and older children. A designation of "all ages" means that the book is a picture book worth reading aloud to all ages.

A FINAL RECOMMENDATION

Many of the recipes are simple and require a minimum of preparation. The new classroom cook should start with the less challenging recipes. It is easy to bring an electric griddle into the classroom to make sourdough pancakes.

Other recipes are more demanding and require the use of a kitchen. Some schools are well equipped for such an undertaking. Some PTAs or student councils have funded a convection oven and a collection of cooking equipment stored on a cart for convenient sharing.

Read each recipe carefully to determine the demands of the preparation with the limitations of your classroom in mind. There is enough variety that all needs can be met.

Suzanne I. Barchers
Patricia C. Marden

Cooking and Safety Tips

COOKING TIPS

1. Read recipe carefully before beginning.

2. Gather ingredients.

3. Gather all utensils, bowls, and other equipment.

4. Turn on the oven to preheat, if needed.

5. Measure exactly.

6. Make sure you have completed each step before going on to the next one.

7. Time any baking or cooking carefully. All baking temperatures are indicated in Fahrenheit.

FOR SAFETY'S SAKE

1. Ask for an adult's help before using the oven or stove. Always use thick, dry potholders to handle hot equipment.

2. Turn off stove and oven when cooking and baking are completed.

3. If grease should catch fire, pour baking soda on the fire. Do not pour water over the flames. If the fire is in a pan, put the lid on to smother the flames.

4. Always tie back long or loose hair when working around the oven or stove. This should also be done with loose sleeves or clothing.

5. Keep hands and face away from steam when cooking liquids over a stove.

6. When cooking with saucepans, always turn the handles so they don't stick out over the edge of the stove.

7. During cooking, allow as few people as possible around hot items. It is best to designate an adult to remain in that area.

8. Sharp instruments should remain on tables when not in use and should be carefully carried to a sink for cleanup by an adult.

9. When peeling vegetables, always move the blade away from your hands.

10. When cutting or chopping use a cutting board to protect counter tops. Always cut away from your hands.

11. Wash knives and other sharp instruments separately from other tools and be careful when wiping the blades.

12. Make sure that your hands are dry whenever plugging in or using electrical appliances.

13. Do not immerse electrical appliances in water when cleaning them. Refer to manufacturer's directions for cleaning.

1
American Indians

Chapter One
Word List

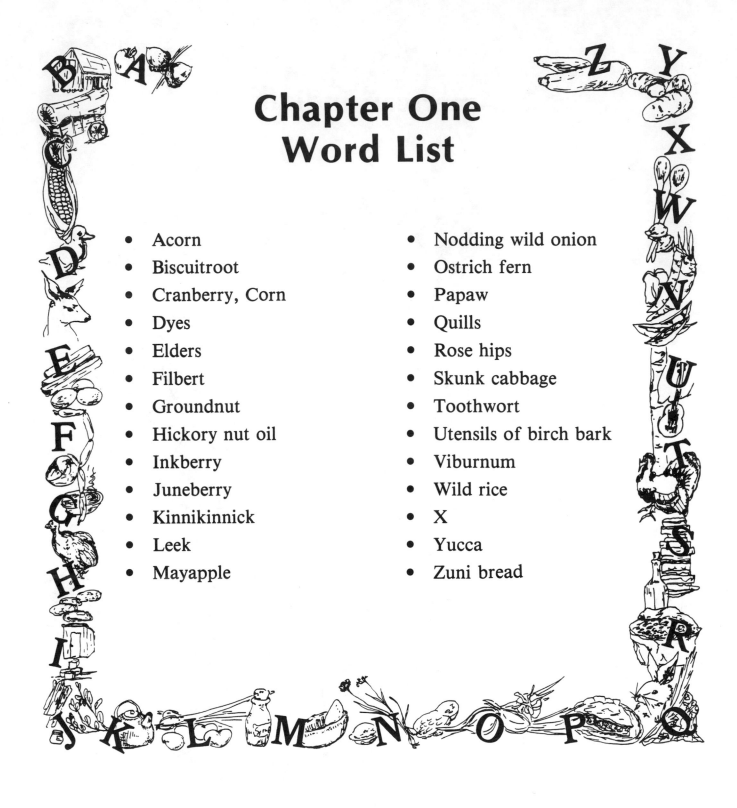

- Acorn
- Biscuitroot
- Cranberry, Corn
- Dyes
- Elders
- Filbert
- Groundnut
- Hickory nut oil
- Inkberry
- Juneberry
- Kinnikinnick
- Leek
- Mayapple
- Nodding wild onion
- Ostrich fern
- Papaw
- Quills
- Rose hips
- Skunk cabbage
- Toothwort
- Utensils of birch bark
- Viburnum
- Wild rice
- X
- Yucca
- Zuni bread

THE INDIAN DIET

When the first settlers arrived in America, the Indians enjoyed an abundant and varied diet, drawing upon over two thousand different plant foods, plus nuts, fruit, fish, seafood, and available game. Their diets were limited only when nature intervened.

They were skilled farmers, adapting their methods to the earth and to the needs of the people. They steadily improved the cultivation of the bean and of corn.

It has been estimated that over 65 percent of our contemporary diet can be traced directly to the contributions of the American Indians. The single most important contribution, however, is corn.

Corn feeds the animals that produce:
    meat
    poultry
    milk
    cheese

Corn oil is found in or is used in the making of or packaging of:
    soap
    insecticides
    mayonnaise
    salad dressings
    monosodium glutamate

Corn syrup is found in or used in the making of:
    candy
    ketchup
    ice cream
    processed meats
    soft drinks
    beer
    gin
    vodka
    sweetened condensed milk

Cornstarch is found in or used in the making of or packaging of:
    puddings
    baby foods
    jams
    pickles
    vinegar
    yeast
    instant coffees
    powdered sugar
    potato flakes
    toothpastes
    cosmetics
    detergents
    dog food
    match heads
    charcoal briquettes

NUTS

The American Indians ate a wide variety of nuts, usually collected by the women and children. The nuts were prepared in many ways, as well as being eaten raw. The following recipes may be used with any nuts that the Indians ate: black walnuts, hickory nuts, hazelnuts, pecans, pine nuts, beech nuts, chestnuts, and acorns.

ROASTED NUTS

Ingredients
Nuts

Steps
1. Shell nuts.
2. Spread nuts in one layer on a cookie sheet.
3. Bake at 300 degrees, stirring often so they don't burn.
4. Bake for about 15 to 20 minutes or until nuts become somewhat crisp. Experiment with the baking time to achieve desired taste.

GROUND NUTS

Ingredients
Nuts

Equipment
Nut grinder

Steps
1. Put a small amount of shelled nuts into nut grinder.
2. Grind nuts into a bowl. This process grates them into dry pieces and not an oily clump.

Library Link 1: What does pawcohiccora mean?

GROUND NUT CAKES

Ingredients
1 cup ground nuts
1 teaspoon vanilla
½ cup maple syrup
½ cup flour

Steps
1. Mix nuts, syrup, and vanilla.
2. Stir in flour.
3. Form dough into 1-inch balls.
4. Place on greased cookie sheets.
5. Bake at 350 degrees for 5 to 10 minutes or until firm and browned.

Makes 15 to 20 cakes.

NUT BUTTER

Ingredients
1 cup nuts
½ teaspoon salt

Steps
1. Grind nuts in a blender until pasty. Some nuts may need a bit of oil added.
2. Stir in salt.

Makes 1 cup.

Library Link 2:   The peanut is an important American food. List some products of the peanut used today.

ACORN MUSH

Ingredients
Acorns
Water

Steps
1. Shell nuts and dry them on baking sheets in the sun for three to five days.
2. Grind nut meats into flour by putting them through a meat grinder or blender.
3. Put acorn flour in a fine strainer.
4. Pour warm water over nut flour.
5. Continue pouring water over flour, increasing the temperature of the water until boiling water is used.
6. Continue pouring water over flour, tasting until flour is sweet instead of bitter.
7. Strain mush.
8. Refrigerate mush until it is used.

ACORN MUSH SOUP

Ingredients
1 quart acorn mush
1 gallon water
Salt

Steps
1. Simmer acorn mush and water until it is the desired thickness.
2. Add salt to taste.

Makes 2 or more quarts, depending on thickness of soup.

Library Link 3:   How were acorns ground before grinders were available?

PEMMICAN

Ingredients
1 pound dried beef or dried buffalo meat
2/3 cup raisins
Suet

Steps
1. Cut dried beef into small chunks.
2. Put beef and raisins in a meat grinder and grind together.
3. Pat beef and raisin mixture into a shallow pan.
4. Melt suet.
5. Pour melted suet over top of mixture to cover.
6. Stir mixture together and allow it to cool.
7. Mixture may be cut into squares to eat.

Serves 4 to 6.

Library Link 4: How was pemmican stored for carrying?

COOKED BEANS

Ingredients
4 cups dried beans (usually navy or pea beans)
1 teaspoon baking soda
½ pound salt pork or ¼ pound bacon
½ cup molasses
2 small onions, chopped

Steps
1. Put beans in large pot and cover with water. Soak overnight.
2. Drain beans.
3. Cover beans with fresh water and bring to a boil. Simmer for 1 hour.
4. Drain beans. Add 6 cups of fresh water, baking soda, and the salt pork or bacon.
5. Simmer for 45 minutes.
6. Pour beans in a greased casserole dish with just enough of the liquid to cover them.
7. Add onions and molasses and stir well.
8. Bake at 350 degrees for 3 to 4 hours or until tender. If beans start to dry out, add more water.

Serves 8.

Library Link 5: Find the earliest record of the existence of beans.

HOMINY

Ingredients
1 quart dried corn
Water
2 tablespoons baking soda
1¼ teaspoons salt
Butter

Steps
1. Wash corn with warm water.
2. Put corn into a stainless steel pan.
3. Add 2 quarts of water and baking soda.
4. Put a lid on the pan and let the mixture sit overnight.
5. Put pan on the stove and bring mixture to a boil.
6. Simmer for 3 hours.
7. Drain the corn and put into cold water.
8. Rub the corn until the hulls are removed.
9. Drain corn and return it to saucepan with 2 more quarts of cold water.
10. Bring to boil.
11. Simmer for 1 hour.
12. Drain, put in cold water, and rub hulls off again.
13. If hulls are not removed at this point, repeat boiling/rubbing process.
14. When hulls have been removed, drain and stir in salt and butter to taste.

Serves 4 to 6.

Library Link 6: In what form was corn first found?

BAKED SQUASH

Ingredients
1 whole acorn squash
2 tablespoons butter or margarine
Salt

Steps
1. Wash squash and cut in half. Clean out seeds.
2. Place squash cut side up on a cookie sheet.
3. Put 1 tablespoon of butter on the top of each half of squash.
4. Bake at 350 degrees about 40 minutes or until squash is soft when pierced with a fork.
5. Sprinkle with salt.

Serves 4 to 6.

Library Link 7: How did American Indians bake squash?

DRIED CORN

Ingredients
3 ears sweet corn

Steps
1. Cut corn kernels from the cobs.
2. Spread kernels one layer deep on cookie sheets.
3. Dry in oven at 175 degrees for several hours until kernels are dried.

Makes approximately 3 cups.

PARCHED CORN

Ingredients
3 tablespoons butter or margarine
3 cups dried corn (see previous recipe)
Salt

Steps
1. Melt butter in a large skillet.
2. Put one layer of corn kernels in the skillet.
3. Heat over medium-high heat, stirring constantly.
4. Kernels are done when they turn brown and puff up (about 4 minutes).
5. Add salt to taste.
6. Repeat until all kernels are cooked.

Library Link 8: Where was the first evidence of corn found?

WILD RICE WITH BLUEBERRIES

Ingredients
1 cup wild rice
2½ cups water
1 teaspoon salt
1 cup blueberries

Steps
1. Wash and drain rice three times.
2. Put rice, water, and salt into a saucepan. Cook over low heat until water is absorbed and rice has softened (about 45 minutes).
3. Stir in blueberries.
4. Serve warm.

Serves 4 to 6.

Library Link 9: Where was wild rice found in North America?

ZUNI SUCCOTASH

Ingredients
½ pound beef, cut into small squares
4 cups water
2 cans corn, drained
2 cans string beans, drained
1 cup sunflower seeds, shelled
Salt and pepper

Steps
1. Boil beef squares in water until tender.
2. Add corn and string beans and heat thoroughly.
3. Mash sunflower seeds by placing seeds between waxed paper and pressing with a rolling pin.
4. Bring beef mixture to a boil again and add mashed seeds, stirring well.
5. Simmer until broth has thickened.
6. Add salt and pepper to taste.

Serves 4 to 6.

Library Link 10: Find several American Indian spellings of succotash.

PIKI

Ingredients
¾ cup cornmeal
½ teaspoon salt
1½ teaspoons sugar
1 tablespoon oil
¾ cup boiling water
1 cup cornmeal
1 tablespoon oil
¾ cup cold water

Steps
1. Mix ¾ cup cornmeal, salt, sugar, and 1 tablespoon oil.
2. Stir in ¾ cup boiling water until just blended.
3. In another bowl, mix 1 cup cornmeal, 1 tablespoon oil, and ¾ cup cold water.
4. Heat a griddle on medium heat.
5. Grease the griddle.
6. Pour the hot-water batter onto the griddle, the size of a small pancake.
7. Immediately pour the cold-water batter over the hot-water batter.
8. Brown on one side, then turn and brown on the other side.

Serves 4.

Library Link 11: Research the eating customs of the American Indians.

BOILED SQUASH PUDDING

Ingredients

2 large acorn squash
½ cup maple syrup or maple sugar
  (brown sugar may be substituted)

3 apples
½ teaspoon salt

Steps

1. Peel squash and cut into small chunks.
2. Put squash in saucepan and add water to about 1 inch deep.
3. Peel, core, and cut apples into chunks.
4. Add apples to squash.
5. Bring water to a boil.
6. Simmer over low heat until squash and apples are soft. Add water if needed.
7. Remove pan from stove.
8. Mash and stir squash and apples.
9. Add maple syrup and stir thoroughly.
10. Serve warm or cold.

Serves 6 to 8.

Library Link 12: Research the agricultural skill of the American Indians.

CRAB-APPLE JELLY

Ingredients

2 pounds crab apples
1¾ cups sugar

4 cups water
1 tablespoon lemon juice

Steps

1. Wash apples and remove the stems.
2. Cut the apples in half.
3. Put apples and water in a large saucepan.
4. Cook over low heat about 30 minutes, until the apples are soft and mushy.
5. Put a colander over a large bowl.
6. Wet a piece of linen or fine cheesecloth. Squeeze out the water and line the colander with the cloth.
7. Pour apple and water mixture, a small amount at a time, onto the linen or cheesecloth.
8. Press mixture through cloth with a large wooden spoon. Remove skin and large pieces that will not go through the cloth.
9. Put all of the strained mixture into a saucepan.
10. Heat to boiling and stir in sugar.
11. Continue heating until temperature reaches 222 degrees on a candy thermometer.
12. If foam forms on top of mixture, skim it off.
13. Remove jelly from heat and stir in lemon juice.
14. Jelly may be eaten when cool or may be preserved in sterilized jars sealed with paraffin.

Library Link 13: The American Indians used crab apples before cultivated apples were brought to America by the colonists. How did the colonists bring their favorite trees to America?

POPCORN BALLS

Note: Later this became a special treat for children during maple syrup boiling time.

Ingredients
3 cups popped popcorn
¾ cup maple syrup

Steps
1. Boil maple syrup in saucepan over medium heat until it reaches 250 degrees or the hard-ball stage, turning hard and crunchy when a drop is dropped into cold water.
2. Pour maple syrup over popcorn in a large bowl. Stir quickly.
3. When syrup cools enough to be handled, roll into balls.
4. Put balls on greased waxed paper until they cool completely.

Makes 5 to 6 medium-sized popcorn balls.

Library Link 14: How did the American Indians pop their popcorn?

BIBLIOGRAPHY—AMERICAN INDIANS

Nonfiction—Series

Glubock, Shirley. *The Art of the North American Indians*. New York: Harper and Row, varying dates. Grades 2 and up.
Photographs of American Indian masks, clothes, pottery, totems, and other museum artifacts demonstrate the range of Indian art. See also titles on the art of the Southwest, Northwest Coast, Plains, Woodlands, and Southeast Indians.

Lepthien, Emilie U. *A New True Book: The Cherokee*. Chicago: Childrens Press, 1985. Grades 1 and up.
Color photographs illustrate these very simple descriptions of the history of the Cherokee. See also titles on the Cheyenne, Chippewa, Choctaw, Navajo, Nez Perce, Pawnee, Seminole, Shoshoni, and Sioux Indians.

Porter, Frank W., editor. *Indians of North America*. New York: Chelsea House Publishers, varying dates. Grades 4 and up.
This extensive series provides colorful descriptions of the histories, lifestyles, customs, and challenges of many different Indian tribes. Photographs, glossaries, and maps make this series especially useful.

Nonfiction—Individual Titles

Aliki. *Corn Is Maize: The Gift of the Indians*. New York: Harper and Row, 1976. All ages.
The history of corn and how it is grown is described. Readers learn about the role of corn in planting and harvest festivals and can even learn what misickquatash is.

Baylor, Byrd. *Before You Came This Way*. Illustrated by Tom Bahti. New York: E. P. Dutton, Inc., 1969. All ages.
Messages from the cliff dwellers, hunters, and other wanderers are described with poetic lines and illustrations made from amatl paper, a handmade bark paper made by the Otomi Indians of Puebla, Mexico.

_____. *They Put on Masks*. Illustrated by Jerry Ingram. New York: Charles Scribner's Sons, 1974. All ages.
Baylor's poetic text tells the reader about the American Indians' use of masks, song, and dance to speak to the gods. Ingram's illustrations are drawn from authentic sources of masks, both ancient and contemporary.

Deur, Lynne. *Indian Chiefs*. Minneapolis, Minn.: Lerner Publications Company, 1972. Grades 4 and up.
Pontiac, Joseph Brant, Tecumseh, Sequoyah, and Crazy Horse are examples of the Indian leaders covered in this book. Black-and-white photographs are included.

Dickinson, Alice. *Taken by the Indians: True Tales of Captivity*. New York: Franklin Watts, Inc., 1976. Grades 6 and up.
The true stories of three men and three women who survived captivity are presented, with some sections in first person. Occasional photographs are included.

Engel, Lorenz. *Among the Plains Indians*. Minneapolis, Minn.: Lerner Publications Company, 1972. Grades 3 and up.
The lithographs of George Catlin and the engravings of Karl Bodmer illustrate this book about the Plains Indians. The text is straightforward and easily read.

Felton, Harold W. *Nancy Ward, Cherokee*. Illustrated by Carolyn Bertrand. New York: Dodd, Mead and Company, 1975. Grades 4 and up.
Nancy Ward believed in peace but supported the colonists during the Revolutionary War, hoping the Cherokees would regain their freedom. Her bravery saved many lives, but though the colonists gained their freedom from England, the Cherokees lost their beloved land.

Freedman, Russell. *Buffalo Hunt*. New York: Holiday House, 1988. Grades 3 and up.
Using museum reproductions of famous paintings, Freedman traces the history of the buffalo, emphasizing its role in the lives of Native Americans.

_____. *Indian Chiefs*. New York: Holiday House, 1987. Grades 3 and up.
Photographs and drawings highlight the stories of these chiefs: Red Cloud of the Oglala Sioux, Quanah Parker of the Comanches, Washakie of the Shoshonis, Joseph of the Nez Perce, Sitting Bull of the Hunkpapa Sioux, and others.

Grimm, William C. *Indian Harvests*. Illustrated by Ronald Himler. New York: McGraw-Hill Book Company, 1973. Grades 3 and up.
American Indians were adept at using all sorts of edible plants. Readers can learn how to use pokeweed, barberry, mustard, milkweed, heath, and many other plants.

Hassrick, Royal B. *The Colorful Story of North American Indians*. London: Octopus Books Limited, 1974. Grades 3 and up.
This oversize book has many black-and-white and color photographs and prints detailing the lives of the Indians. Topic headings include Origins, Desert Dwellers, Woodland Indians, Farmers of the Midwest, Warriors of the Plains, Gatherers of the Far West, Seafarers of the Northwest Coast, Hunters of the North, and Indians of Today.

Hirsch, S. Carl. *Famous American Indians of the Plains*. Illustrated by Lorence Bjorklund. Chicago: Rand McNally and Company, 1973. Grades 3 and up.
Line drawings and occasional color illustrations highlight stories of the nomadic life sometimes known as the "horse culture."

Hofsinde, Robert. *Indian Hunting*. New York: William Morrow and Company, 1962. Grades 3 and up.
The American Indians relied on animals for more than just food. Hofsinde describes the Indians' hunting methods, weapons, and ceremonials.

_____. *Indian Picture Writing*. New York: William Morrow and Company, 1959. All ages.
Simple drawings for American Indian picture writing are organized thematically. Letters written in picture writing challenge readers to attempt translations.

_____. *Indians at Home*. New York: William Morrow and Company, 1964. Grades 3 and up.
American Indians did not all live in tepees. Hofsinde (Gray-Wolf) describes the variety of homes maintained by the Indians of North America.

Hunt, W. Ben. *The Complete How-to Book of Indiancraft*. New York: Collier Books, 1973. Grades 4 and up.
Dozens of authentic projects are described with drawings, photos, and charts. Lore and history are interspersed with directions for various crafts.

_____. *Indian Crafts and Lore*. New York: Western Publishing Company, 1954. All ages.
American Indian names, lore, dress, symbols, makeup, dances, drumming, tepees, and totem poles are described with text and colorful drawings.

Jacobson, Daniel. *The Gatherers*. Illustrated by Richard Cuffari. New York: Franklin Watts, Inc., 1977. Grades 4 and up.
The course of history that affected the tribes from ancient times to the present is described with text and drawings about various American Indians.

Johnston, Johanna. *The Indians and the Strangers*. Illustrated by Rocco Negri. New York: Dodd, Mead and Company, 1972. Grades 2 and up.
Woodcuts illustrate the simple text that discusses the takeover of the Indian lands by white men. Stories are included of Squanto, Powhatan, Massasoit, Philip, Tammany, Pontiac, Sacajawea, Tecumseh, and others.

Kirk, Ruth, and Richard D. Daugherty. *Hunters of the Whale: An Adventure in Northwest Coast Archaeology*. Photographs by Ruth Kirk and Louis Kirk. New York: William Morrow and Company, 1974. Grades 5 and up.
Ozette, a prehistoric Indian village, is excavated, and Daugherty assists with the documentation of the artifacts. Photographs of the process and intriguing text provide an instructive book.

Lavine, Sigmund A. *The Games the Indians Played*. New York: Dodd, Mead and Company, 1974. Grades 4 and up.
History and culture are intertwined with the descriptions of games of chance, dexterity, and children. Black-and-white photographs are included.

_____. *The Houses the Indians Built*. New York: Dodd, Mead and Company, 1975. Grades 3 and up.
Lavine describes the temporary shelters of bark, brush, grass, reeds, or skin, as well as the permanent buildings of the Indians of the Southwest and Central America. Photographs and prints are included.

Levenson, Dorothy. *Homesteaders and Indians*. New York: Franklin Watts, Inc., 1971. Grades 3 and up.
    The story of the gradual takeover of the homelands of the Indians and the homesteaders who claimed the land is described in straightforward text. Drawings or photographs made during the nineteenth century enhance the text.

Malloy, Anne. *Wampum*. New York: Hastings House Publishers, 1977. Grades 4 and up.
    Wampum is not just a form of money. It is also an atonement, communication, and a form of sacred record keeping. Prints and photographs illustrate Malloy's recounting of the significance of wampum in the past and present.

Mason, Bernard S. *Dances and Stories of the American Indian*. Photographs by Paul Boris and others. Illustrations by Frederic H. Koch. New York: A. S. Barnes and Company, 1944. Teacher resource.
    Though intended for adults interested in teaching children about Indian dance, this book could be used by older children researching dances. Through the dance, one can learn about rituals, masks, clothing, and customs.

May, Robin. *Plains Indians of North America*. Vero Beach, Fla.: Rourke Publications, Inc., 1987. Grades 3 and up.
    Color photographs illustrate this relatively simple discussion of the life of the Plains Indians.

Morrison, Dorothy Nafus. *Chief Sarah: Sarah Winnemucca's Fight for Indian Rights*. New York: Atheneum, 1980. Grades 4 and up.
    Sarah fought for American Indian rights as a lecturer, writer, educator, and lobbyist.

Oritz, Simon. *The People Shall Continue*. Illustrated by Sharol Graves. San Francisco: Children's Book Press, 1988. All ages.
    The stories of the American Indians' origins, their struggle to adapt to a new way of life, and their desire to unite with all people are described with poetic words and colorful illustrations.

Parish, Peggy. *Let's Be Indians*. Illustrated by Arnold Lobel. New York: Harper and Row, 1962. All ages.
    Line drawings illustrate a variety of projects suitable for young children. Examples are headbands, moccasins, jewelry, corn-husk dolls, cradle boards, salt clay, and pottery.

Santrey, Laurence. *Pocahontas*. Illustrated by David Wenzel. Mahwah, N.J.: Troll Associates, 1985. Grades 2 and up.
    Simple text and colorful illustrations make this a good introduction to the story of Pocahontas.

Seigel, Beatrice. *Indians of the Woodland before and after the Pilgrims*. Illustrated by Baptiste Bayhylle Shunatona, Jr. New York: Walker and Company, 1972. Grades 3 and up.
    Each chapter begins with a simple question about the Indians, such as, "What did they look like?" Black-and-white line drawings provide insights into their lives.

Skold, Betty Westrom. *Sacagawea: The Story of an American Indian*. Minneapolis, Minn.: Dillon Press, Inc., 1978. Grades 5 and up.
    Sacagawea (Sacajawea) is traded to Toussaint Charbonneau, a French-Canadian fur trader, by a tribe that had held her hostage. Charbonneau is hired as the interpreter for the Lewis and Clark expedition, and the woman proves to be an invaluable aide.

Stein, R. Conrad. *The Story of The Trail of Tears*. Illustrated by David J. Catrow III. Chicago: Childrens Press, 1985. Grades 3 and up.
This is the story of the Cherokees' valiant struggle to preserve their territories and tribes.

_____. *The Story of Wounded Knee*. Illustrated by David J. Catrow III. Chicago: Childrens Press, 1983. Grades 3 and up.
The death of Sitting Bull and the tragedy at Wounded Knee are described.

Supree, Burton. *Bear's Heart: Scenes from the Life of a Cheyenne Artist of One Hundred Years Ago with Pictures by Himself*. New York: J. B. Lippincott, 1977. Grades 3 and up.
A large number of Plains Indians were imprisoned in Florida by the U.S. Army. One Cheyenne, Bear's Heart, was given a notebook, and he used it to record his life's story in pictures. The tragic story is told in carefully worded text to accompany his drawings.

Tomkins, William. *Indian Sign Language*. New York: Dover Publications, Inc., 1964. All ages.
In addition to the drawings and explanations of sign language, Tomkins describes pictography, ideography, and smoke signals of the Sioux and Ojibway tribes.

Yue, Charlotte. *The Tipi: A Centre of Native American Life*. New York: Alfred A. Knopf, Inc., 1984. Grades 5 and up.
Black-and-white drawings complement this straightforward account of the history of the tipis (tepees) of the Plains Indians.

Wolfson, Evelyn. *From Abenaki to Zuni: A Dictionary of Native American Tribes*. Illustrated by William Sauts Bock. New York: Walker and Company, 1988. Grades 3 and up.
The locations, dwellings, food, clothing, and transportation are discussed for sixty-eight North American Indian tribes. The maps, symbols, labeled drawings, glossary, and index provide an excellent research tool.

_____. *Growing up Indian*. Illustrated by William Sauts Bock. New York: Walker and Company, 1986. Grades 3 and up.
Questions about virtually every aspect of an American Indian child's life are asked and answered. General topics are babies, toddlers, schools, families, toys and games, becoming an adult, and Indian children of today.

Fiction

Armer, Laura Adams. *Waterless Mountain*. Illustrated by Sidney Armer and Laura Adams Armer. New York: David McKay Company, Inc., 1931. Grades 4 and up.
This story of a Navaho boy's training in the ancient religion of his people is set against the arid landscape of northern Arizona.

Baker, Olaf. *Where the Buffaloes Begin*. Illustrated by Stephen Gammell. New York: Frederick Warne, 1981. Grades 2 and up.
Little Wolf, a courageous American Indian boy, searches for the source of the buffaloes, but finds that it is up to him to save his people.

Beatty, Patricia. *Wait for Me, Watch for Me, Eula Bee*. New York: William Morrow and Company, 1978. Grades 5 and up.

Lewallen and Eula Bee are captured by Comanches in Texas in 1860. Lewallen's efforts to rescue four-year-old Eula Bee provide an intriguing story of frontier life.

Benchley, Nathaniel. *Only Earth and Sky Last Forever*. New York: Harper and Row, 1972. Grades 5 and up.

Based on true accounts, Benchley tells the powerful story of a young Indian's decision to join Crazy Horse and fight for his beliefs.

Bulla, Clyde Robert. *Indian Hill*. Illustrated by James J. Spanfeller. New York: Thomas Y. Crowell, 1963. Grades 2 and up.

Kee moves from a hogan on an American Indian reservation to a city apartment. The family's adjustment is difficult, but Kee helps with the process.

_____. *Pocahontas and the Strangers*. Illustrated by Peter Burchard. New York: Thomas Y. Crowell, 1971. Grades 3 and up.

Bulla tells the story of Pocahontas and her struggle to have faith in her people and the white people. Her marriage to John Rolfe and her experiences in Jamestown and England are described.

Byars, Betsy. *Trouble River*. Illustrated by Rocco Negri. New York: Puffin, 1989. Grades 4 and up.

Dewey and his grandmother escape the Indians by rafting down a challenging river.

Colver, Anne. *Bread-and-Butter Indian*. Illustrated by Garth Williams. New York: Holt, Rinehart and Winston, 1964. Grades 1 and up.

Barbara, a young child, has been warned about the Indians in the woods. When she meets one, she becomes his friend by sharing her bread and butter. When she is later captured by an Indian, her friend comes to her rescue. Based on the author's husband's family history. See also *Bread-and-Butter Journey* in chapter 4.

DePaola, Tomie. *The Legend of the Bluebonnet: An Old Tale of Texas*. New York: G. P. Putnam's Sons, 1983. All ages.

She-Who-Is-Alone is a young girl of the Comanche tribe who makes a great sacrifice to save her people. This is the legend of the bluebonnet flowers.

Edmonds, Walter D. *The Matchlock Gun*. Illustrated by Paul Lantz. New York: Dodd, Mead and Company, 1941. Grades 4 and up.

This early Newbery Medal book tells the story of an Indian attack on colonial settlers from the colonists' point of view.

Esbenson, Barbara Juster. *The Star Maiden: An Ojibway Tale*. Illustrated by Helen K. Davie. Boston: Little, Brown and Company, Inc., 1988. Grades 1 and up.

This is an Indian tale of the maiden who tires of the sky and decides to adopt an earthly form, choosing the water lily.

Gardiner, John R. *Stone Fox*. New York: Thomas Y. Crowell, 1980. Grades 2 and up.

An American Indian who is reclaiming lost land and a boy who is trying to save his grandfather's farm are adversaries in a dogsled race. The equally valid causes for winning the prize provide a gripping story.

Goble, Paul. *The Girl Who Loved Wild Horses*. Scarsdale, N.Y.: Bradbury Press, 1978. All grades.
    An American Indian girl has a special relationship with horses. When a storm startles the herd, she takes a horse's mane and rides off with the herd forever.

_____. *Her Seven Brothers*. Scarsdale, N.Y.: Bradbury Press, 1988. Grades 3 and up.
    Goble uses stunning illustrations and lyrical prose to retell the Cheyenne legend of the big dipper.

_____. *Lone Bull's Horse Raid*. New York: Bradbury Press, 1973. Grades 3 and up.
    A young Oglala Sioux tells how he and his best friend join a horse-raiding party to steal from the Crow Indians.

Gregory, Kristiana. *Jenny of the Tetons*. New York: Harcourt Brace Jovanovich, 1989. Grades 4 and up.
    Carrie is wounded and alone after an Indian attack. She is cared for by a trapper whose wife is a Shoshoni Indian, Jenny. Carrie begins to respect Jenny and the Indians' regard for the land.

Hood, Flora. *The Turquoise Horse: Prose and Poetry of the American Indian*. Illustrated by Marylou Reifsnyder. New York: G. P. Putnam's Sons, 1972. All ages.
    Drawings in turquoise, tan, and black illustrate the poetry of the Indians.

Hotze, Sollace. *A Circle Unbroken*. New York: Clarion Books, 1988. Grades 4 and up.
    Rachel was captured by American Indians in 1838 and was lovingly raised as the chief's daughter. When she was recaptured by her father, a stern minister, she longed to return to the tribe.

Lampman, Evelyn Sibley. *Cayuse Courage*. New York: Harcourt Brace and World, 1970. Grades 5 and up.
    Samuel Little Pony is torn between his respect for Dr. Marcus Whitman, who saved his life, and his Indian heritage. See *Stout-Hearted Seven...* (annotated in chapter 4) for an excellent supplement to this story, which ends in the Whitman Massacre.

_____. *The Potlatch Family*. New York: Atheneum, 1976. Grades 6 and up.
    Plum Longor, a Pacific Coast Chinook, feels others dislike her because of her dark skin and alcoholic father. The return of her brother results in the revival of their customs, bringing dignity to the Indians and their community.

_____. *Squaw Man's Son*. New York: Atheneum, 1978. Grades 5 and up.
    Billy, who is half white and half American Indian, leaves his home in Oregon and joins the Madocs, who eventually fight the whites. Billy is captured and released to his father. He realizes he doesn't fit in either world.

_____. *The Year of the Small Shadow*. New York: Harcourt Brace Jovanovich, 1971. Grades 5 and up.
    When his father is sent to prison for stealing a horse, Small Shadow is sent to stay with the white lawyer who helped his father. His experiences help others overcome their fears of the American Indians.

Leech, Jay, and Zane Spencer. *Bright Fawn and Me*. Illustrated by Glo Coalson. New York: Thomas Y. Crowell, 1979. Grades 1 and up.
    A Cheyenne family is participating in an intertribal fair in the late 1800s, and an older sister does not appreciate having to care for her younger sister.

McGovern, Ann. *Little Wolf*. Illustrated by Nola Langner. New York: Scholastic Book Services, 1965. Grades 1 and up.
    Little Wolf is brave, but he does not want to hurt his animal friends. He finds dignity as a healer.

McGraw, Eloise Jarvis. *Moccasin Trail*. New York: Coward McCann and Geoghegan, 1952. Grades 5 and up.
When a white boy is attacked by a bear, he is rescued by the Crow Indians, who raise him. Eventually he meets his family and must reconcile the two worlds.

Mitchell, Barbara. *Tomohawks and Trombones*. Illustrated by George Overlie. Minneapolis, Minn.: Carolrhoda Books, 1982. Grades 1 and up.
Based on a true incident, this is the story of how Delaware Indians were frightened away by the blaring of trombones.

Monjo, Ferdinand. *Indian Summer*. Illustrated by Anita Lobel. New York: Harper and Row, 1968. Grades 2 and up.
When a father joins George Washington, the family must defend itself against Indian attack.

O'Dell, Scott. *Sing Down the Moon*. Boston: Houghton Mifflin Company, 1970. Grades 3 and up.
The injustices of the move of the Navajos from Arizona to Fort Sumner, New Mexico, are detailed in this suspenseful novel.

_____. *Streams to the River, River to the Sea: A Novel of Sacagawea*. Boston: Houghton Mifflin Company, 1986. Grades 5 and up.
The journey of Lewis and Clark is told through Sacajawea's eyes. O'Dell gives new insights into her role.

_____. *Zia*. Boston: Houghton Mifflin Company, 1976. Grades 4 and up.
Zia embarks on a search for her aunt, moving to a Santa Barbara mission and challenging the sea in an attempt to rescue Karana. (Sequel to *Island of the Blue Dolphins*, see chapter 11 for description.)

Rockwood, Joyce. *Groundhog's Horse*. Illustrated by Victor Kalin. New York: Holt, 1978. Grades 4 and up.
Groundhog, an eleven-year-old Cherokee, must rescue his stolen horse alone.

_____. *To Spoil the Sun*. New York: Holt, 1976. Grades 5 and up.
Through Rain Dove's life, the reader learns of the problems brought to the Indians by the white man.

Sobol, Rose. *Woman Chief*. New York: Dial Books, Inc., 1976. Grades 4 and up.
Raised as a Crow Indian, Lonesome Star is trained as a hunter and warrior, eventually achieving the status of chief.

Speare, Elizabeth George. *Calico Captive*. New York: Dell Publishing Company, Inc., 1957. Grades 5 and up.
Miriam is falling in love in 1754 when she is captured by Indians and forced to march north to be sold to the French in Montreal. Her story is fictionalized, based on accounts of the capture and journey of Miriam's relative, Susanna Johnson.

_____. *The Sign of the Beaver*. Boston: Houghton Mifflin Company, 1983. Grades 3 and up.
A young boy survives two seasons in the Northeast woods while his father returns to their former home for his wife and younger children. Unexpected help from Indians leads to a dilemma when the Indians are forced out of their lands.

Spencer, Paula Underwood. *Who Speaks for Wolf: A Native American Learning Story*. Illustrated by Frank Howell. Austin, Texas: Tribe of Two Press, 1983. All ages.

This story, preserved in oral form, reminds the reader of the importance of learning from and remembering the past. Howell's soft illustrations make this a wonderful read-aloud story.

Steele, Mary O., and William O. Steele. *The Eye in the Forest*. New York: E. P. Dutton, Inc., 1975. Grades 4 and up.

While searching for the Sacred Eye, Kontu is captured by a primitive tribe. This story is based on Native American Indians living before the arrival of European settlers.

Steele, William O. *The Man with the Silver Eyes*. New York: Harcourt Brace Jovanovich, 1976. Grades 4 and up.

Talatu is forced to spend time with Shinn, a pale-eyed white man, and Talatu finds his courage through the experience.

Strete, Craig Kee. *When Grandfather Journeys into Winter*. Illustrated by Hal Frenck. New York: Greenwillow Books, 1979. Grades 2 and up.

Tayhua gives his grandson, Little Thunder, the prize stallion he earned, in addition to a proud heritage of love and courage.

Udry, Janice May. *The Sunflower Garden*. Irvington, N.Y.: Harvey House, 1969. Grades 2 and up.

Pipsa saves her baby brother from a rattlesnake and wins her father's admiration.

Wallin, Luke. *In the Shadow of the Wind*. Scarsdale, N.Y.: Bradbury Press, 1984. Grades 5 and up.

It is the early 1800s and a young American Indian girl, Pine Creek, and a white man, Caleb McElroy, must reconcile their love for each other in a period of changing values.

Wheeler, M. J. *First Came the Indians*. Illustrated by James Houston. New York: Atheneum, 1983. All ages.

Simple poetry describes six North American Indian tribes: Creek, Iroquois, Chippewa, Sioux, Makah, and Hopi.

2
The Colonial Period

Mayflower food supplies:

- Crackers
- Cheese
- Butter
- Bacon
- Salted fish
- Root vegetables
- Dried fruit

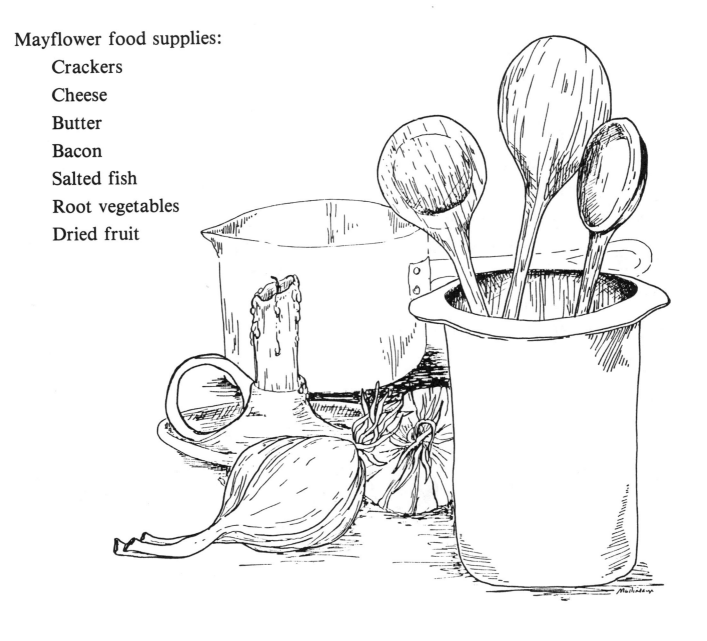

Chapter Two
Word List

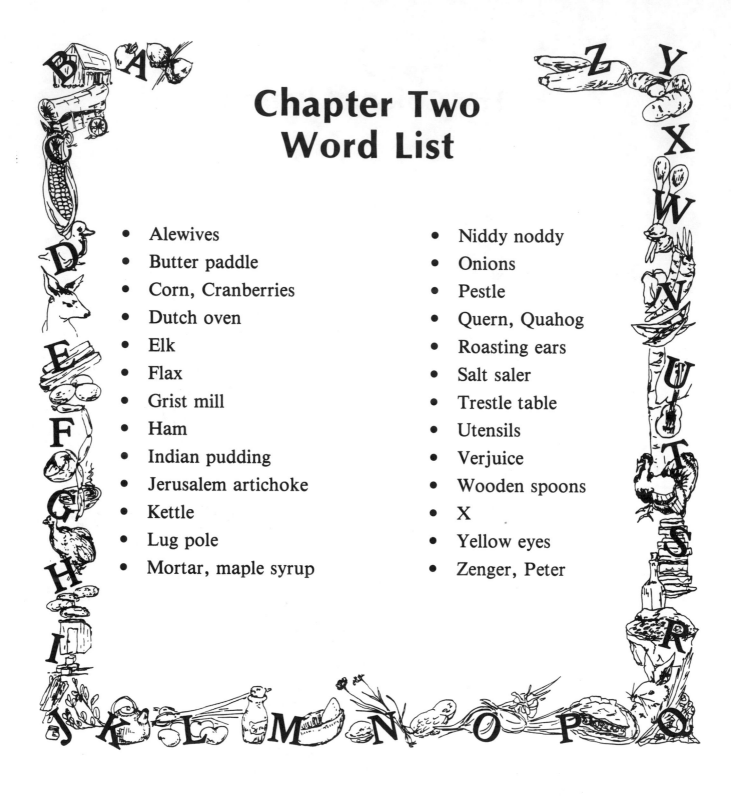

- Alewives
- Butter paddle
- Corn, Cranberries
- Dutch oven
- Elk
- Flax
- Grist mill
- Ham
- Indian pudding
- Jerusalem artichoke
- Kettle
- Lug pole
- Mortar, maple syrup

- Niddy noddy
- Onions
- Pestle
- Quern, Quahog
- Roasting ears
- Salt saler
- Trestle table
- Utensils
- Verjuice
- Wooden spoons
- X
- Yellow eyes
- Zenger, Peter

PORRIDGE

The early colonists often had porridge, or oatmeal, for breakfast. They served it with hasty pudding (see following recipe).

Ingredients
4 cups water
½ teaspoon salt
2 cups old-fashioned oats
Molasses or maple sugar

Steps
1. Pour water in saucepan and bring to a boil over medium-high heat.
2. Stir in salt and oats.
3. Turn heat down to medium. Cook and stir the mixture for about 10 minutes.
4. Cover pan and remove from heat.
5. Let stand until thickened (5 to 10 minutes).
6. Serve with molasses or maple sugar.

Serves 6.

Library Link 1: Where do oats come from? What other uses were there for oats? Why was it important to the early colonists to have a good supply of oats?

HASTY PUDDING

Hasty pudding, or cornmeal mush, was a staple of the early colonists diet. They served hasty pudding warm with molasses over it for breakfast. For lunch and dinner they cooled and sliced it.

Ingredients
2 cups water
⅓ cup cornmeal
½ teaspoon salt
Molasses or maple syrup

Steps
1. Put water in the bottom and 2 cups water in the top of a double boiler and boil over medium heat.
2. Stir in cornmeal and salt.
3. Cook until thick, about 1 hour, stirring occasionally.
4. Serve warm with molasses or maple syrup. Or cool and then slice.

Serves 4.

Library Link 2: What word did the American Indians use for corn? Did the early colonists use corn before they came to America? Why or why not?

CORNMEAL PUDDING

Ingredients
4½ cups milk
⅓ cup cornmeal
½ cup molasses
¾ teaspoon salt

Steps
1. Heat the milk in a saucepan until it is scalded.
2. Place cornmeal in the top of a double boiler.
3. Slowly pour in the scalded milk, stirring constantly.
4. Cook the mixture in the double boiler over medium heat for 20 minutes.
5. Add molasses and salt and stir well.
6. Butter a baking dish.
7. Pour the cornmeal mixture into the baking dish.
8. Bake mixture in the oven at 325 degrees for 1½ to 2 hours or until firm.

Serves 4 to 6.

Library Link 3: Our cornmeal looks like flour and comes in a bag or carton. How did the early colonists prepare cornmeal? Why did they use cornmeal instead of wheat flour?

JOHNNYCAKES OR JOURNEY CAKES

Ingredients
1 egg
2 cups cornmeal
¾ teaspoon salt
1½ cups milk
Butter
Powdered sugar, if desired

Steps
1. Beat egg.
2. Stir in cornmeal, salt, and milk.
3. Drop spoonfuls of batter on a well greased, hot griddle.
4. Fry until brown on both sides.
5. Serve hot with butter and/or powdered sugar.

Makes 10 to 12.

Library Link 4: How did the colonists' diet change from what they ate in England? Why?

CORN STICKS

Ingredients
1¼ cups milk
1 cup cornmeal
¾ cup flour
¾ teaspoon salt
3 teaspoons baking powder
⅓ cup molasses
2 eggs, beaten
2 tablespoons oil
2 tablespoons butter, melted

Steps
1. Heat milk in saucepan until it is scalded.
2. Put cornmeal in a mixing bowl and pour the hot milk over it.
3. Mix thoroughly and then let it cool to lukewarm.
4. Add the flour, salt, and baking powder to the cooled cornmeal mixture and stir well.
5. Stir in the molasses, beaten eggs, oil, and melted butter.
6. Pour the mixture into a well greased bread-stick pan.
7. Bake at 400 degrees for about 20 minutes.

Makes approximately 12 corn sticks.

Library Link 5: This recipe uses molasses as a sweetener; however, such sweeteners were scarce in the 1600s. Find out how the Pilgrims sweetened their desserts and vegetables when they had no sugar, honey, or molasses.

BUTTER

Ingredients
Heavy whipping cream
Salt, to taste

Steps
1. Take cream out of refrigerator about 1 hour before making butter.
2. Pour cream into a glass jar that has a tight-fitting lid. Fill only half full.
3. Shake jar until curd (solid) separates completely from whey (liquid).
4. Pour whey into a separate container. This may be drunk as buttermilk.
5. Pour curd into a strainer and let drain for several minutes until all liquid is drained off.
6. Place curd into a bowl and stir in salt.
7. Use butter as desired.

Library Link 6: Keep track of how much butter your family consumes in one week. Decide how many hours would be used to make your family a week's worth of butter based on how long it took your class to make butter. Then decide how much time it would take to obtain the necessary ingredients for butter.

BLACK BEAN SOUP

Ingredients
2 cups black beans
3 quarts water
1½ onions, sliced
3 bay leaves
3 stalks celery, chopped
½ pound salt pork
Salt and pepper, to taste

Steps
1. Soak beans in the water overnight.
2. The next morning, add the rest of the ingredients and cook over low heat.
3. Cook until beans are soft and mushy, adding more water as needed.
4. Press entire bean mixture through a coarse sieve, pushing through all possible ingredients.
5. Add water, salt, and pepper as necessary.
6. Reheat mixture to serve.

Serves 4 to 6.

Library Link 7:   To what family does the bean plant belong? What other commonly eaten plants belong to this family? Why did the colonists rely on these plants?

SQUASH SOUP

Ingredients
2 large acorn squash
1½ cups boiling water
4½ cups milk
3 tablespoons butter
Salt and pepper, to taste

Steps
1. Peel the squash, cut in half, remove the seeds, and cut it into small pieces.
2. Cook the squash in boiling water until it is soft.
3. Scald the milk.
4. Mash the squash and then stir in the scalded milk.
5. Heat, but do not let mixture boil.
6. Stir in the butter, salt, and pepper.

Serves 4 to 6.

Library Link 8:   When is squash harvested? Of what importance is the harvesting season to the early colonists?

FISH CHOWDER

Ingredients

3 tablespoons shortening
1 onion, sliced thin
2½ pounds fresh fish
    (cod, haddock, etc.)
3 raw potatoes, peeled and
    chopped into small pieces

Water
2 tablespoons melted butter
2 tablespoons flour
3 cups milk
1½ teaspoons salt
¼ teaspoon pepper

Steps

1. Melt shortening in a large saucepan.
2. Cook onion in it until the onion is tender.
3. Remove skin and bones from the fish.
4. Cut fish into small pieces.
5. Add fish and potatoes to saucepan and cover with water.
6. Cover and cook over low heat until potatoes are tender.
7. Mix butter and flour in a bowl.
8. Add a little of the hot fish broth to flour mixture and stir.
9. Pour flour mixture into broth and stir.
10. Add milk, salt, and pepper.
11. Stir and simmer for a few minutes.

Makes approximately 3 quarts.

Library Link 9: A chowder is a kind of soup or stew. What is another popular kind of chowder? In what areas of the United States are chowders most popular? Why?

SUCCOTASH

Ingredients

2 cups fresh lima beans
3½ cups fresh corn kernels
5 tablespoons butter
Salt and pepper, to taste

Steps

1. Place lima beans in boiling salted water.
2. Cover and cook about 30 minutes or until tender.
3. Add the corn and stir.
4. Pour off extra water so that remaining water just covers corn.
5. Cook over low heat about 5 to 10 minutes or until most of the water is evaporated.
6. Stir in butter, salt, and pepper.

Serves 6 to 8.

Library Link 10: The Pilgrims learned how to make succotash from the Indians, who grew the beans and corn together in the same patch. How could this dish be made available in the winter? How would the preparation change?

PILGRIMS' DESSERT (STEWED PUMPKIN)

Ingredients
Fresh pumpkin, peeled, seeded, and cut into cubes
Water
Ginger (1 teaspoon for medium saucepan of pumpkin)
Molasses

Steps
1. Put pumpkin cubes in a saucepan.
2. Add water to about 1 inch deep in the pan.
3. Cover and cook over medium heat until pumpkin is very soft. Stir occasionally.
4. Stir in ginger to taste.
5. Let pumpkin cool slightly. Serve in bowls with molasses.

Serves 4 to 6, depending on size of pumpkin.

Library Link 11: How did the early colonists learn about pumpkins? Pumpkins have been featured in many stories and poems throughout our history. Find stories that have pumpkins in them.

BERRY INK

Ingredients
⅔ cup ripe fresh or frozen berries (blueberries, strawberries, raspberries, etc.)
½ teaspoon salt
½ teaspoon vinegar

Steps
1. Fill a strainer with berries and place it over a bowl.
2. Use a large spoon to crush the berries, letting the juice strain into the bowl.
3. Keep adding berries to the strainer until all berries have been crushed.
4. Throw the berry pulp away.
5. Add the salt and vinegar to the berry juice and stir.
6. Store berry ink in a jar with a lid.

Library Link 12: The colonists not only made their own inks but made their own quills. Find out how this was done.

NUT INK

Ingredients

6 whole walnut shells
½ teaspoon vinegar

¾ cup water
½ teaspoon salt

Steps

1. Crush the empty shells by wrapping them in a rag and smashing them with a hammer.
2. Put the crushed shells in a pan and add the water.
3. Bring the water to a boil.
4. Turn the heat down and let the water simmer for about 45 minutes, until it turns dark brown.
5. Let the mixture cool. Pour it through a strainer into a jar.
6. Add the vinegar and salt to the ink.
7. Use nut ink with quill or wooden pens.

Library Link 13: Colonists also made their own paper. Find out how this was done. Find examples of contemporary artists who have returned to the art of making paper. (Ask your art teacher for help.) Consider making paper for an extra project.

HAND SOAP

Caution: Lye use requires adult supervision. Lye flakes are poisonous and can burn skin. If lye touches skin, immediately flood area with water. Do *not* use an aluminum pan. Soap making may produce smoke and irritating fumes.

Ingredients

32 ounces olive oil
14 ounces vegetable shortening
6 ounces lye flakes
16 ounces water

Equipment

Newspapers
Rubber gloves
Cooking thermometer
Shoe box or shallow pan

Steps

1. Cover table with newspaper. Wear rubber gloves.
2. Put oil and shortening in a large glass or stainless steel pot (not aluminum).
3. Heat mixture on lowest setting. Stir with wooden spoon.
4. In a small glass or stainless steel pot, dissolve lye flakes in 16 ounces of water.
5. Use a cooking thermometer to see that the mixtures in both pans reach 96 degrees. Lye and water mixture will get hotter; let it cool down to 96 degrees.
6. Slowly pour lye mixture into oil mixture, stirring constantly.
7. Stir until thick, about 15 minutes.
8. Line a shoe box or shallow pan with waxed paper or plastic wrap.
9. Pour soap mixture into box or pan.
10. Let soap harden for 24 hours.
11. Cut the soap brick into smaller pieces.
12. Allow soap to sit for at least 2 weeks before using it.

Library Link 14: The colonists used all available resources to survive. Ashes were used to make lye, and nuts and berries were used for ink. Use the library to find other examples of how the colonists utilized and conserved materials.

DIPPED CANDLES

Caution: Keep baking soda handy to smother flames should paraffin ignite.

Ingredients
1 pound paraffin
Cotton string

Equipment
Newspaper
2 tall tin cans (1-pound coffee cans work well)
Saucepan
Fork

Steps
1. Spread newspaper on table.
2. Fill 1 tin can about ⅔ full of water and place in a saucepan. Fill the other can with cold water.
3. Fill the saucepan about ½ full of water and put over medium heat on the stove.
4. As the water in the saucepan begins to boil, add chunks of paraffin to the tin can inside the saucepan until the can is almost full.
5. As the wax melts, it forms a layer on top of the water. The wax needs to be just the right temperature. If it is too hot it will slide off the string. If it is too cool it will be too thick for dipping. Keep the pan on the stove at a low heat.
6. Cut a piece of string 2 times as long as the can.
7. Lay the string over the prongs of a fork so that both sides hang down equally. Take the portion that lies over the fork and weave it among the prongs to hold the string in place.
8. Dip the string into the can until it touches the bottom.
9. Pull the string out of the can and dip it in the can of cold water to harden.
10. Continue dipping the string into the wax and then cold water until candles are as thick as desired.
11. Trim the wicks to about ½ inch before burning candles.

Makes 6 medium candles.

Library Link 15: We can buy paraffin for making candles. How did the colonists obtain the materials for making candles?

MOLDED CANDLES

Caution: Keep baking soda handy to smother flames should paraffin ignite.

Ingredients
Paraffin
Cotton string

Equipment
Cardboard containers
Double boiler
Pencil

Steps
1. Melt paraffin in top of double boiler over low to medium heat.
2. Cut string about 4 inches longer than cardboard container.
3. Cut off the top of the container. Poke a hole in the bottom and thread the string through hole. On the outside of the carton (bottom), knot the string to hold it in place.
4. Turn container right side up and tie the other end of string onto a pencil that has been laid across the top of the container. The string should be taut.
5. Pour melted wax into the cardboard container, almost to the top.
6. After the wax has cooled and hardened thoroughly, remove from container by dipping it in hot water for about 10 seconds and inverting the container.
7. Remove pencil and cut off excess string.

Library Link 16: How would the colonists obtain molds for their molded candles? Would all colonists have molded candles? Why or why not?

CANDLE CLOCK

Equipment
2 or more fat candles the same height and thickness
2 jar lids
Pencil or permanent marker

Steps
1. Use the jar lids as candle holders by dripping wax in the center of them and standing the candles up in the wax.
2. Place the 2 candles (on jar lids) side by side.
3. Have a clock nearby to measure the time.
4. Light 1 of the candles. After 1 hour, mark the other candle at exactly the remaining height of the burning candle. Make a mark the same way after each hour until the first candle has burned all the way down.
5. Write a number by each mark on the candle to mark the hours.
6. Use the marked candle to mark other candles, making your own candle clocks.

Library Link 17: Figure out how many candles your family would need each week to have three hours of candlelight every evening.

BIBLIOGRAPHY—THE COLONIAL PERIOD

Nonfiction—Series

Colonial Histories. Nashville, Tenn.: Thomas Nelson, Inc., Publishers, varying dates. Teacher resource or
older students.
   This series traces the histories of the 13 colonies from their earliest days through the Revolutionary
War. Photographs, prints, maps, documents, and personal accounts enhance the narratives.

The Colony Series. New York: Franklin Watts, Inc., varying dates. Grades 3 and up.
   This series features individual books about the 13 colonies: Delaware, Georgia, Maryland, Massachu-
setts, New Hampshire, Connecticut, New Jersey, New York, North Carolina, Pennsylvania, Rhode Island,
South Carolina, and Virginia. The authors vary.

Fisher, Leonard Everett. *Colonial American Craftsmen*. New York: Franklin Watts, Inc., varying dates.
All ages.
   Each of the following craftsmen is a title in the series, simply presented in under 50 pages: Wigmaker,
Weaver, Tanners, Silversmiths, Shoemakers, Shipbuilders, School Masters, Printers, Potters, Peddlers,
Papermakers, Architects, Homemakers, Hatters, Glassmakers, Doctors, Cabinet Makers, and
Blacksmiths.

Nonfiction—Individual Titles

Anderson, Joan. *The First Thanksgiving Feast*. Photographed by George Ancona. New York: Clarion
Books, 1984. All ages.
   The Thanksgiving feast, recreated at the outdoor living history museum, Plimoth Plantation,
Massachusetts, is beautifully photographed in black and white. Representative residents are profiled.

Barth, Edna. *Turkeys, Pilgrims, and Indian Corn: The Story of the Thanksgiving Symbols*. Illustrated by
Ursula Arndt. New York: Clarion Books, 1975. Grades 3 and up.
   Barth's book is an excellent collection of facts about Thanksgiving, describing not only the Pilgrims'
feast, but also related celebrations. Topics range from Pilgrim faces and houses to Indian corn, cranberries,
and Tom Turkey.

Behrens, June, and Pauline Brower. *Colonial Farm*. Chicago: Childrens Press, 1976. Grades 1 and up.
   Color photographs illustrate the day-to-day life of a typical colonial farm family. Based on the Turkey
Run Farm near McLean, Virginia.

Campbell, Elizabeth A. *Jamestown: The Beginning*. Illustrated by William Sauts Bock. Boston: Little,
Brown and Company, Inc., 1974. Grades 3 and up.
   Jamestown's founding is described in relatively simple text and pen, ink, and wash drawings.

Colloms, Brenda. *The Mayflower Pilgrims*. New York: St. Martin's Press, 1973. Grades 2 and up.
   Drawings, photographs, and brief discussions depict the Pilgrims' flight, journey, and settling in North
America.

Cowie, Leonard W. *The Pilgrim Fathers*. New York: G. P. Putnam's Sons, 1972. Grades 4 and up.
   Photographs and pictures highlight this documentary, recreating the voyage of the *Mayflower* and the
settling in the new land.

Faber, Doris. *Colony Leader: Anne Hutchinson*. Champaign, Ill.: Garrard Publishing Company, 1970. Grades 3 and up.
    Anne is banished from the Puritan church because she defends the right of freedom of conscience. She settles in Rhode Island and Long Island, facing many challenges to pursue her dream of continuing her father's work as a minister.

Fisher, Margaret, and Mary Jane Fowler. *Colonial America: English Colonies*. Grand Rapids, Mich.: Gateway Press, Inc., 1988. Grades 3 and up.
    Black-and-white photos and prints, plus relatively simple text, give the student background in the areas of colonial homes.

Fritz, Jean. *What's the Big Idea, Ben Franklin?* Illustrated by Margot Tomes. New York: Putnam Publishing Group, 1976. Grades 3 and up.
    Ben Franklin's eccentricities and inventions are discussed in this lively biography. The amusing illustrations add interest to the reading.

Gemming, Elizabeth. *The Cranberry Book*. New York: Coward-McCann, Inc., 1983. Grades 4 and up.
    Gemming describes the contribution of the cranberry to the diet of the colonists, as well as its cultivation and harvesting.

Glubok, Shirley. *The Art of Colonial America*. New York: Macmillan Publishing Company, 1970. All ages.
    Glubok presents through photos, prints, and text the art of early America: pewter, silver, pottery, glass, furniture, portraits, and paintings of homes.

Groh, Lynn. *The Pilgrims: Brave Settlers of Plymouth*. Illustrated by Frank Vaughn. Champaign, Ill.: Garrard Publishing Company, 1968. Grades 2 and up.
    Sketches and black-and-white photographs accompany this account of why the Pilgrims left England, the settling of Plymouth, the challenges, the hardships, and the routine of everyday life.

Kalman, Bobbie. *Early Schools*. New York: Crabtree Publishing Company, 1982. Grades 3 and up.
    This particularly enjoyable book explores in words and pictures the lessons, rules, punishments, routines, and supplies of early American schools.

Langdon, William Chauncey. *Everyday Things in American Life 1607-1776*. New York: Charles Scribner's Sons, 1965. Grades 3 and up.
    This is a vast resource for anyone interested in learning about the very fabric of everyday life in the colonies. Houses, utensils, trading posts, home crafts, pewter, silver, money, glass, furniture, and ships are but a few examples of the subjects covered by Langdon. Though harder to read than the indicated grade level, the detailed index, fine illustrations, and relatively straightforward style make this an excellent resource for beginning research.

Loeb, Robert H., Jr. *Meet the Real Pilgrims: Everyday Life on Plimoth Plantation in 1627*. Garden City, N.Y.: Doubleday and Company, Inc., 1979. Grades 3 and up.
    Black-and-white photographs and fascinating text guide the reader through a visit of a working replica of 1627 Plimoth (Plymouth).

_____. *New England Village: Everyday Life in 1810*. Garden City, N.Y.: Doubleday and Company, Inc., 1976. Grades 2 and up.
    Using photographs from Old Sturbridge Village and Old Slater Mill, Loeb explains the workings of the farm, shops, schools, and other aspects of colonial life.

May, Robin. *A Colonial American Merchant*. Illustrated by Mark Bergin. Vero Beach, Fla.: Rourke Enterprises, Inc., 1986. Grades 2 and up.
Color pictures from a variety of sources lend authenticity to this simple text. It is well organized, with segments depicting a colonial merchant's life up until the Boston Tea Party.

Palmer, Ann. *Growing Up in Colonial America*. East Sussex, U.K.: Wayland Publishers, Inc., 1978. Grades 2 and up.
This is a good resource for beginning researchers. Topics are neatly divided into families; parents and children; children at work; schools and learning; amusements; apprentices, servants, and slaves; and growing up. Illustrations include drawings, woodcuts, and photographs.

Perl, Lila. *Slumps, Grunts, and Snickerdoodles: What Colonial America Ate and Why*. Illustrated by Richard Cuffari. Boston, Mass.: Houghton Mifflin Company, 1975. Grades 4 and up.
The importance of food in colonial times is thoroughly discussed by Perl. The key recipes of the period are included.

Raskin, Joseph, and Edith Raskin. *The Newcomers: Ten Tales of American Immigrants*. Illustrated by Kurt Werth. New York: Lothrop Lee and Shepard Company, 1974. Grades 3 and up.
Using diaries, court records, and historical accounts, the authors have constructed 10 tales of immigrants from all over the world. Ocean-born Mary, Snow-Shoe Thompson, Asser Levy, and others will entertain and educate readers.

Sewall, Marcia. *The Pilgrims of Plimoth*. New York: Atheneum, 1986. All ages.
Sewall's lovely paintings enhance her description of the Plimoth (Plymouth) Pilgrims.

Sloane, Eric. *ABC Book of Early Americana: A Sketchbook of Antiquities and American Firsts*. Garden City, N.Y.: Doubleday and Company, Inc., 1963. All ages.
This beautifully illustrated ABC book provides a fascinating history of the early days of America. Full of trivia, it is a useful reference book, especially for the early reader.

Smith, E. Brooks, and Robert Meredith. *The Coming of the Pilgrims*. Illustrated by Leonard Everett Fisher. Boston: Little, Brown and Company, Inc., 1964. Grades 2 and up.
The Pilgrims' story is told from Governor Bradford's firsthand account. Bradford kept records of all the challenges faced by these brave people. Fisher's illustrations are in black and white with touches of blue and orange.

Speare, Elizabeth George. *Life in Colonial America*. New York: Random House, 1963. Grades 4 and up.
Beginning with the Jamestown Colony in 1607, Speare provides a rich overview of colonial life. The routines of religion, home life, defense, school, trades, and holidays are explored. There is a liberal sprinkling of drawings and photographs.

Szekeres, Cyndy. *Long Ago*. New York: McGraw-Hill Book Company, 1977. Grades K through 3.
Full-color illustrations of make-believe costumed animals accompany a simple text that provides insights into the life of "long ago." The animals living as settlers make this appealing to the youngest and fun for the earliest readers.

Tunis, Edwin. *Colonial Living*. New York: Thomas Y. Crowell, 1957. Grades 3 and up.
   This is an excellent resource book for students doing research on any period from the sixteenth to eighteenth century. The thorough table of contents makes this exceptionally easy to reference. Line drawings add interest and information.

_____. *The Tavern at the Ferry*. New York: Thomas Y. Crowell, 1973. Grades 4 and up.
   In 1687 Henry Baker assisted a stranger across the Delaware River. During the next 100 years, the role of Baker's Ferry and Tavern became increasingly important in the events leading up to the Revolutionary War. By recreating taverns through pencil and wash drawings, Tunis provides an unusual slice of colonial history.

Weisgard, Leonard. *The Plymouth Thanksgiving*. Garden City, N.Y.: Doubleday and Company, Inc., 1967. Grades 1 and up.
   This simple narrative provides a fine first look at the story of the Pilgrims. An intriguing section lists all the passengers from the *Mayflower*.

Nonfiction—Other

Colonial Sing: Games and Dances. Williamsburg, Va.: Colonial Williamsburg Foundation, 1977. All ages.
   For a tape or record and booklet on teaching colonial songs, games, and dances, write for ordering information to the Colonial Williamsburg Foundation, AV Distribution, Williamsburg, VA 23185.

Fiction

Adler, David A. *Remember Betsy Floss and Other Colonial American Riddles*. Illustrated by John Wallner. New York: Bantam, 1987. All ages.
   This collection of silly riddles, such as, "Who was given thread but flossed her teeth instead?" provides a pleasant diversion during the study of colonial times.

Avi. *Night Journey*. New York: Pantheon Books, 1979. Grades 4 and up.
   Peter York is a young orphan being cared for by a stern master. Peter becomes involved with an indentured servant, and their escape is a story of courage and suspense.

Benchley, Nathaniel. *George, the Drummer Boy*. Illustrated by Don Bolognese. New York: Harper and Row, 1977. Grades 1 and up.
   From the British viewpoint comes a story of a drummer boy who is on a frightening mission during the Battles of Lexington and Concord.

Blos, Joan. *A Gathering of Days: A New England Girl's Journal, 1830-32*. New York: Charles Scribner's Sons, 1979. Grades 5 and up.
   Catherine Hall uses her journal to work through the challenges she faces after her mother dies and her father decides to remarry.

Bulla, Clyde Robert. *John Billington, Friend of Squanto*. New York: Thomas Y. Crowell, 1956. Grades 2 and up.
   This is the story of John's journey on the *Mayflower* and his growing friendship with Squanto.

_____. *A Lion to Guard Us*. Illustrated by Michele Chessare. New York: Scholastic Book Services, 1981. Grades 3 and up.
   It is the early 1600s, and Jemmy, Meg, and Amanda must make their way from London to America to join their father.

Clapp, Patricia. *Constance: A Story of Early Plymouth*. New York: Lothrop Lee and Shepard Company, 1968. Grades 5 and up.
The first entry in Constance's journal is November 9, 1620, the day America is sighted. The next six years tell about her growth as a young lady in the settlement of Plymouth.

Dalgliesh, Alice. *The Courage of Sarah Noble*. New York: Charles Scribner's Sons, 1954. Grades 1 and up.
Sarah is eight years old in 1707, living with her father in Connecticut while he builds their family's log cabin. When he returns to Massachusetts for the rest of the family, Sarah stays with an Indian family.

_____. *The Thanksgiving Story*. Illustrated by Helen Sewell. New York: Charles Scribner's Sons, 1954. All ages.
This is the story of the Hopkins family during their first year in the Plymouth Colony.

Daugherty, James. *The Landing of the Pilgrims*. New York: Random House, 1950. Grades 4 and up.
Daugherty uses the journals of the Pilgrims to retell the story of their incredible journey and struggles in the New World.

Hays, Wilma Pitchford. *Pilgrim Thanksgiving*. Illustrated by Leonard Weisgard. Eau Claire, Wis.: E. M. Hale and Company, 1955. Grades 2 and up.
Damaris and her family had come to America on the *Mayflower*. This is their story of the first Thanksgiving feast.

Latham, Jean. *This Dear-Bought Land*. Illustrated by Jacob Landau. New York: Harper and Row, 1957. Grades 5 and up.
This is the story of the settlement of Jamestown and of Captain John Smith.

Lawson, Robert. *Ben and Me: A New and Astonishing Life of Benjamin Franklin as Written by His Good Mouse Amos*. Boston: Little, Brown and Company, Inc., 1939. Grades 4 and up.
Amos, the oldest of 26 mice that lived in the vestry of Old Christ Church, gives a true accounting of the adventures of Benjamin Franklin.

Lee, Beverly Haskell. *The Secret of Van Rink's Cellar*. Minneapolis, Minn.: Lerner Publications Company, 1979. Grades 3 and up.
Sarah, eleven years old, and Stephen, nine years old, are living in a seemingly haunted house in colonial New York. When their mother becomes ill, they learn that she is a spy for General Washington. They carry on for her, discovering the identity of their ghost.

Lenski, Lois. *Puritan Adventure*. Philadelphia: J. B. Lippincott, 1944. Grades 4 and up.
This is the story of the Partridge family living in the Massachusetts Bay Colony.

Lobel, Arnold. *On the Day Peter Stuyvesant Sailed into Town*. New York: Harper and Row, 1971. Grades 1 and up.
Stuyvesant was the new governor of New Netherland in 1647. When he arrived he was horrified by the conditions and set out to change the future of the city.

McCurdy, Michael. *Hannah's Farm: The Seasons on an Early American Homestead*. New York: Holiday House, 1988. All ages.
The seasons of a typical nineteenth-century New England homestead, Morgan Farm, are explored through Hannah's life. McCurdy's wood engravings suit the content of the book.

Monjo, F. N. *The House in Stink Alley: A Story about the Pilgrims in Holland*. Illustrated by Robert Quackenbush. New York: Holt, Rinehart and Winston, 1977. Grades 3 and up.
    Preceding the arrival of the Pilgrims in America, this story tells of Pilgrim refugees after they left England and took refuge in Holland.

Speare, Elizabeth George. *The Witch of Blackbird Pond*. New York: Dell Publishing Company, Inc., 1972. Grades 5 and up.
    When Kit moves from the Caribbean to the New England coast, she is unprepared for the drab existence, treatment of suspected witches, and general loneliness.

Spier, Peter. *The Legend of New Amsterdam*. Garden City, N.Y.: Doubleday and Company, Inc., 1979. Grades K and up.
    Spier's full-color picture book describes the customs, jobs, and people of New Amsterdam in the 1660s. The story of a widow, Crazy Annie, lends interest.

Watson, Sally. *Jade*. New York: Holt, Rinehart and Winston, 1969. Grades 4 and up.
    Jade is 16 in the 1700s. She hates slavery and is caught freeing a shipload of slaves. A pirate, Anne Bonney, rescues Jade, who joins the pirate crew.

3
The Revolutionary War

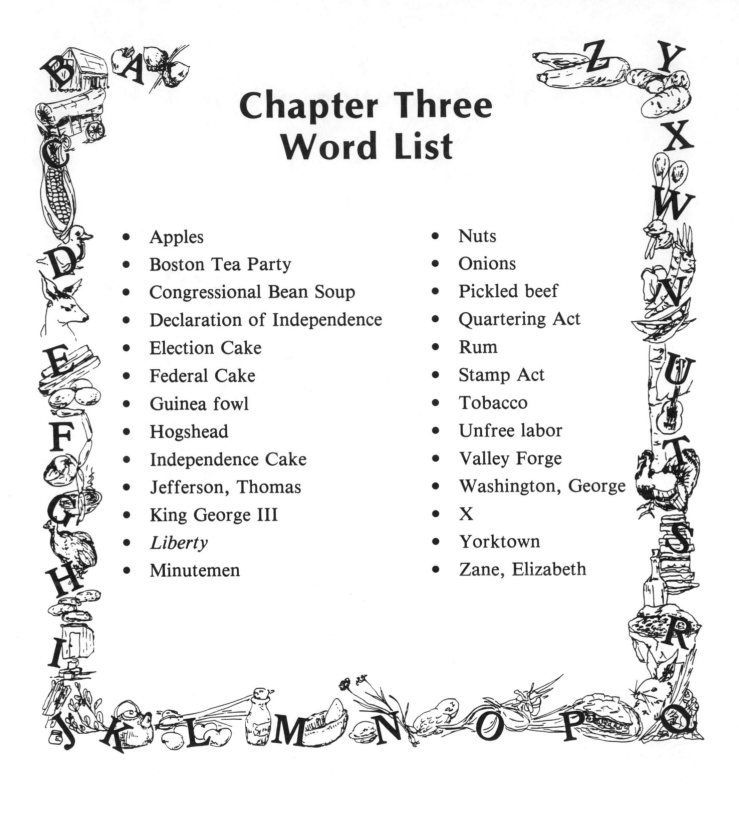

Chapter Three
Word List

- Apples
- Boston Tea Party
- Congressional Bean Soup
- Declaration of Independence
- Election Cake
- Federal Cake
- Guinea fowl
- Hogshead
- Independence Cake
- Jefferson, Thomas
- King George III
- *Liberty*
- Minutemen
- Nuts
- Onions
- Pickled beef
- Quartering Act
- Rum
- Stamp Act
- Tobacco
- Unfree labor
- Valley Forge
- Washington, George
- X
- Yorktown
- Zane, Elizabeth

TAPPING TREES FOR MAPLE SYRUP

The Indians originally taught the settlers how to tap maple trees for the sap in order to make maple syrup and maple sugar. Trees must be tapped in early spring, just as the snow begins to thaw. Sugar maple or black maple trees provide the largest quantities of sap. A spout is hammered into the tree, creating about a half inch hole, and a bucket is hung from it. After the sap is collected in the bucket, it is boiled until most of the water has evaporated and a thick syrup is left.

MAPLE SYRUP CANDY

Ingredients

Maple syrup   Snow

Steps
1. Cook maple syrup over medium heat in a saucepan until it reaches 275 degrees or the hard-ball stage (forms a hard ball when dropped in a cup of cold water).
2. Fill large cake pan with a mound of clean snow.
3. Slowly pour cooked syrup over snow, dribbling it in thin strips.
4. Let syrup cool.

Library Link 1: What does "sap's rising!" mean? Read *Sugaring Time* by Kathryn Lasky (see bibliography) and write a report about making maple syrup today.

SWEET POTATO CAKE

Ingredients

1 cup butter or margarine, softened   ¾ teaspoon baking soda
2 cups sugar   1 teaspoon cinnamon
4 eggs   ½ teaspoon nutmeg
2¾ cups cooked,   ½ teaspoon allspice
   mashed sweet potatoes   ¼ teaspoon salt
3 cups flour   2 teaspoons vanilla
2 teaspoons baking powder   1 cup chopped nuts (optional)

Steps
1. Cream butter and stir in sugar.
2. Add eggs one at a time, beating well after each one.
3. Add sweet potato and mix thoroughly.
4. In a separate bowl, mix the flour, baking powder, baking soda, cinnamon, nutmeg, allspice, and salt.
5. Slowly add flour mixture to sweet potato mixture, stirring well.
6. Stir in vanilla.
7. Add nuts, if desired.
8. Pour batter into a greased, 10-inch tube pan.
9. Bake for 1 hour and 10 minutes at 350 degrees or until done.

Serves 10 to 12.

Library Link 2: This recipe has several spices in it: vanilla, cinnamon, nutmeg, and allspice. Why are spices important in history? Why were spices heavily used in meat?

SWEET POTATO PUDDING

Ingredients
2 cups raw, grated sweet potato
1½ cups water
⅓ cup sugar
¼ teaspoon cinnamon
¼ teaspoon allspice
4 tablespoons melted margarine

Steps
1. Combine the potato with the water, sugar, cinnamon, and allspice.
2. Stir in the melted margarine.
3. Grease a 1-quart casserole dish.
4. Pour the mixture into the dish.
5. Cover the dish with aluminum foil and bake at 350 degrees for 30 minutes.
6. Uncover the dish and bake for about 30 minutes more or until a knife inserted in the center comes out clean.

Serves 6.

Library Link 3: How do sweet potatoes differ from white potatoes? Why did the colonists eat so many sweet potatoes?

CORNMEAL SPOON BREAD

Ingredients
1¾ cups milk
¼ teaspoon salt
⅔ cup cornmeal
3 tablespoons butter
2 eggs

Steps
1. Boil milk in a medium-sized saucepan.
2. Add salt.
3. Stir in cornmeal and continue to stir until mixture thickens.
4. Add butter and stir.
5. Remove mixture from heat.
6. Beat eggs well and then stir into cornmeal mixture.
7. Butter a 9-inch square baking pan.
8. Pour mixture into the pan.
9. Bake at 375 degrees for 1 hour.

Makes 9 1-inch square pieces.

Library Link 4: Today we set our ovens to the temperature we need to bake our foods. The colonists did not have electric or gas ovens. How did they bake? What problems would they have? How might they try to solve them?

INDIAN PUDDING

Ingredients

¼ cup cornmeal
1½ cups cold milk
2½ cups heated milk
4 tablespoons margarine

¾ cup molasses
½ teaspoon cinnamon
¼ teaspoon salt
2 well beaten eggs

Steps

1. In the bottom half of a double boiler, heat water until it boils.
2. In the top of the double boiler, stir cornmeal into 1 cup of the cold milk.
3. Stir in the 2½ cups of heated milk.
4. Cook and stir until smooth.
5. Cover the pan.
6. Lower heat so that the water simmers lightly. Cook for 25 to 30 minutes.
7. Remove from heat.
8. Stir in the rest of the ingredients.
9. Pour the mixture into a buttered 2-quart baking pan.
10. Pour the remaining cold milk on top.
11. Bake at 350 degrees for about 1 hour or until firm.

Serves 4 to 6.

Library Link 5:   Puddings are used in folk and fairy tales and nursery rhymes. Find as many stories with puddings in them as you can. Extra challenge: What is a pudding stone?

CHESS PIE

Ingredients

1 9-inch pastry shell, unbaked
½ cup margarine or butter
1 cup brown sugar
3 eggs
⅓ cup evaporated milk

¾ cup chopped nuts (pecans or walnuts)
¾ cup raisins
½ cup chopped dates
½ teaspoon vanilla
⅓ cup orange juice

Steps

1. Cream the butter.
2. Stir in sugar and eggs until smooth and creamy.
3. Stir in milk, nuts, raisins, dates, vanilla, and orange juice.
4. Pour mixture in pie shell.
5. Bake pie for 10 minutes at 450 degrees.
6. Reduce heat to 325 degrees and bake about 25 minutes.

Serves 8.

Library Link 6:   Find out why this pie is called chess pie. (Hint: Chess is believed to have come from the word chest.)

VIRGINIA POUND CAKE

Ingredients
2 cups butter
2 cups sugar
9 eggs
1½ teaspoons vanilla
½ teaspoon nutmeg
2 tablespoons orange juice
4 cups flour

Steps
1. Cream butter.
2. Using an electric mixer, beat in sugar until smooth and creamy (or beat by hand for 5 minutes).
3. Beat eggs in a separate bowl until thick and light yellow.
4. Add eggs to butter mixture and mix very well (or beat by hand for 5 minutes).
5. Beat in vanilla, nutmeg, and orange juice.
6. While mixer is running, beat in flour, a small amount at a time (or beat very well by hand).
7. Grease 2 9-inch loaf pans.
8. Pour half of the mixture into each pan.
9. Bake at 325 degrees for about 1 hour or until a toothpick inserted in the center comes out clean.

Serves 15 to 20.

Library Link 7: Find out why this cake is called pound cake. In early 1774, why did women have tea parties without tea?

COTTAGE CHEESE

Ingredients
½ gallon skim milk
⅓ cup fresh cultured buttermilk
Water

Equipment
1 dairy thermometer
1 long stainless steel knife
1 large pan or kettle
Rack to fit in the bottom of the large pan
Stainless steel or enamel bowl or pan that fits into the large pan
Muslin sack or cheesecloth

Steps
1. Let skim milk and buttermilk sit out until they reach room temperature (70 to 75 degrees).
2. Stir buttermilk into skim milk in stainless steel pan.
3. Let stand 12 to 14 hours until clabbered (soured and separated).
4. Cut through clabbered milk with a stainless steel knife at ½ inch intervals, first down, then across, then diagonally. Cut all the way to the bottom. This is the curd.
5. Let stand for 10 minutes.
6. Add 1 quart of 100 degree water to curd.
7. Set the pan with the curd in it on the rack in the larger pan that has been one-third filled with water.
8. Heat until the curd reaches 100 degrees. Keep it at this temperature for about 45 minutes, stirring every 5 minutes.
9. As you stir, the whey (liquid) will be forced out and the curds will settle to the bottom.
10. Curds are done cooking when they break between the fingers without leaving a milky liquid on the fingers.
11. Pour the curds and whey carefully into the muslin sack and rinse with cold water.
12. Let drain until liquid stops dripping.
13. A small amount of cream may be stirred into curds if they are too dry.
14. Cover and store in the refrigerator.

Serves 6.

Library Link 8: What famous nursery rhyme talks about curds and whey? When were the first cows brought to America?

FRUIT JELLY

Ingredients
3 pounds of fruit, to yield about 4 cups of juice. (No pineapple or quince.)
¾ cup sugar for each cup of juice

Equipment
Large saucepan
Colander
Cheesecloth
Jars
Paraffin
Small saucepan
2 large bowls
Teakettle full of water
Hot pad mittens (to lift jars of hot water)

Steps
1. Wash the fruit and cut it into small pieces. (Do not peel or core.)
2. Put fruit in saucepan and cook until it creates juice, in about 5 to 15 minutes. If necessary, add some water to keep fruit from burning.
3. Strain fruit through a colander into a bowl.
4. Wash colander and place it over the second large bowl.
5. Pour the juice from the first bowl through several layers of cheesecloth draped over the colander.
6. Let the juice drip through for about an hour.
7. Measure juice by the cup into the saucepan.
8. Boil juice for 5 minutes.
9. Add ¾ cup of sugar for each cup of fruit juice.
10. Boil mixture for 15 to 30 minutes or until mixture jells or thickens. Test to see if it has jelled by putting a few drops in the freezer for a few minutes to see if it gets thick when cooled.
11. Boil water in the teakettle.
12. Pour boiling water into jars, and then immediately empty the jars and fill with jelly.
13. Melt paraffin in a small saucepan over very low heat.
14. Pour about ½ inch of melted paraffin over the top of each jar of jelly. Let it cool.
15. Jars are now sealed and can be stored in a cool, dry place.

Library Link 9: What kinds of berries did the colonists find available to them?

APPLE BUTTER

Ingredients
Apples (enough to equal 4 cups of sieved fruit)
¾ cup sugar or honey
¾ teaspoon cinnamon
2 tablespoons margarine or butter (melted)

Steps
1. Wash and quarter apples.
2. Remove cores and stems.
3. Put apples in a large kettle.
4. Add about 1 inch water.
5. Cover kettle and cook until fruit is soft.
6. Put apples through a food mill or colander.
7. Measure 4 cups of fruit into a 9 by 13-inch baking pan.
8. Add sugar or honey, cinnamon, and margarine. Stir well.
9. Bake at 300 degrees.
10. Stir every 30 minutes.
11. Bake until thick.

Library Link 10: Johnny Appleseed was born in 1774. What was his real name? When did he begin planting apple trees?

BIBLIOGRAPHY—THE REVOLUTIONARY WAR

Nonfiction

Adler, David A. *A Picture Book of George Washington*. Illustrated by John Wallner and Alexandra Wallner. New York: Holiday House, 1989. All ages.
This simple, colorful picture book gives an overview of the life of George Washington. This is a good read-aloud for the very young.

Alderman, Clifford Lindsey. *The Dark Eagle: The Story of Benedict Arnold*. New York: Macmillan Publishing Company, 1976. Grades 5 and up.
Before Arnold became infamous as a traitor, he was considered a great Revolutionary War general. This biography provides insights into both his character and the war.

Anticaglia, Elizabeth. *Heroines of '76*. New York: Walker and Company, 1975. Grades 3 and up.
Heroic women and their contributions to the Revolutionary War are presented: Margaret Cochran Corbin, Mary Ludwig Hays McCauley, Frederika Charlotte Louise von Riesdesel, Deborah Sampson, Molly Brant, Lydia Darragh, Betsy Ross, Nancy Hart, Elizabeth Zane, Mercy Otis Warren, Phyllis Wheatley, Ann Lee, and Patience Lovel Wright.

Clinton, Susan. *The Story of the Green Mountain Boys*. Chicago: Childrens Press, 1987. Grades 3 and up.
Led by Ethan Allen, the Green Mountain Boys fought against the British in various northern areas of the colonies. The text is straightforward, with photographs and art of the period.

Clyne, Patricia Edwards. *Patriots in Petticoats*. New York: Dodd, Mead and Company, 1976. Grades 4 and up.
  Thirty heroic women are portrayed. The book follows each portrayal with a description of historic sites that can be seen today.

d'Aulaire, Ingri, and Edgar d'Aulaire. *Benjamin Franklin*. Garden City, N.Y.: Doubleday and Company, Inc., 1950. Grades 2 and up.
  The accomplishments of Benjamin Franklin are told with simple but highly decorated text. Many of Poor Richard's sayings are included, with Pennsylvania Dutch decorations.

Davis, Burke. *Black Heroes of the American Revolution*. New York: Harcourt Brace Jovanovich, 1976. Grades 3 and up.
  Black Revolutionary War heroes risked their lives, hoping this was the first step on the path to freedom. This book includes black-and-white prints and portraits of the period.

Evans, R. E. *The American War of Independence*. Minneapolis, Minn.: Lerner Publications Company, 1977. Grades 3 and up.
  Maps, black-and-white illustrations, and photographs illustrate the course of the war. This is a good source for the beginning researcher.

Fisher, Leonard Everett. *Liberty Book*. Garden City, N.Y.: Doubleday and Company, Inc., 1976. All ages.
  Liberty is celebrated in this oversized picture book of quotations, poems, songs, and flags.

_____. *Picture Book of Revolutionary War Heroes*. Harrisburg, Penn.: Stackpole Books, 1970. Grades 3 and up.
  Fifty war heroes (two are female) are profiled. Fisher uses blue-and-white drawings.

Fritz, Jean. *And Then What Happened, Paul Revere?* Illustrated by Margot Tomes. New York: Coward McCann and Geoghegan, 1973. Grades 2 and up.
  Fritz intersperses the story of Paul Revere with humorous tidbits and anecdotes. For example, Paul's children were named Deborah, Paul, Sarah, Mary, Frances, and Elizabeth (from his first wife), and Joshua, Joseph, Harriet, Maria, and John (from his second wife).

_____. *Can't You Make Them Behave, King George?* Illustrated by Tomie DePaola. New York: Coward McCann and Geoghegan, 1982. Grades 3 and up.
  Americans often assume King George the Third was primarily a tyrant. Fritz's biography provides a more balanced, while entertaining, view of King George.

_____. *Shh! We're Writing the Constitution*. Illustrated by Tomie DePaola. New York: G. P. Putnam's Sons, 1987. Grades 3 and up.
  Writing the Constitution was a necessary challenge, and Fritz describes the process with humorous and engrossing details.

_____. *Where Was Patrick Henry on the 29th of May?* Illustrated by Margot Tomes. New York: Coward McCann and Geoghegan, 1975. Grades 3 and up.
  Another humorous look at one of the well known Revolutionary War figures is provided by Fritz. Henry's flair for drama and his ability to capitalize on any situation he encountered is described with intriguing detail.

_____. *Why Don't You Get a Horse, Sam Adams?* Illustrated by Trina Schart Hyman. New York: Coward McCann and Geoghegan, 1974. Grades 3 and up.

Sam Adams was willing to dress up a bit when talking to people about the English government and the need to fight for independence, but he drew the line at riding a horse.

_____. *Will You Sign Here, John Hancock?* Illustrated by Trina Schart Hyman. New York: Coward McCann and Geoghegan, 1975. Grades 3 and up.

John Hancock's refusal to pay taxes to King George and his general flamboyancy, including his signing of the Declaration of Independence, are described.

Gauch, Patricia Lee. *This Time, Tempe Wick?* New York: Coward McCann and Geoghegan, 1974. Grades 2 and up.

Tempe Wick may be a girl, but she lived through the Revolutionary War and refused to let the soldiers take her beloved horse.

Giblin, James Cross. *Fireworks, Picnics, and Flags: The Story of the Fourth of July Symbols*. Illustrated by Ursula Arndt. New York: Clarion Books, 1983. Grades 3 and up.

The history of the events surrounding the Revolutionary War is presented through a discussion of the symbols of the Fourth of July. Included are chapters on the Centennial Exhibition of 1876 and the Bicentennial of 1976.

Grant, Anne. *Danbury's Burning! The Story of Sybil Ludington's Ride*. Illustrated by Pat Howell. New York: David McKay Company, Inc., 1976. Grades 1 and up.

Paul Revere was 40 when he made his historic 16-mile ride. Sybil was 16 when she rode nearly 40 miles to alert her neighbors to the burning of Danbury. Colorful illustrations highlight her exciting ride.

Griffin, Judith Berry. *Phoebe and the General*. Illustrated by Margot Tomes. New York: Coward McCann and Geoghegan, 1977. Grades 2 and up.

Phoebe, a young, free, black girl, serves as a spy to prevent the assassination of General George Washington. This exciting, true tale dramatizes the role of one young person in the forging of our government.

Haley, Gail E. *Jack Jouett's Ride*. New York: Viking Press, 1973. All ages.

Color linoleum cuts and simple text tell the story of Jack Jouett's four-mile nighttime ride to warn the leaders of the Revolutionary War that Tarleton's Raiders were on their way to capture them.

Lasky, Kathryn. *Sugaring Time*. Photographs by Christopher G. Knight. New York: Macmillan Publishing Company, 1983. Grades 2 and up.

Black-and-white photographs highlight this factual narrative of the process of gathering maple syrup. Though set in contemporary times, the process is not that different from that of years ago.

Levy, Elizabeth. *If You Were There When They Signed the Constitution*. Illustrated by Richard Rosenblum. New York: Scholastic Book Services, 1987. Grades 3 and up.

In question-and-answer form, Levy explains the importance of the Constitution to the United States.

Luckhardt, Mildred Corell, editor. *Brave Journey: Launching of the United States*. Illustrated by Tom Armstrong. Nashville, Tenn.: Abingdon Press, 1975. Grades 4 and up.

These are the stories of the participants of the war—some famous, some unknown, some old, some young. This would be particularly good for the teacher to selectively read aloud throughout a unit of study.

Maestro, Betsy, and Giulio Maestro. *A More Perfect Union: The Story of Our Constitution*. New York: Lothrop Lee and Shepard Company, 1987. Grades 1 and up.
The events surrounding the writing and ratification of the Constitution are described with text and large watercolors.

McGovern, Ann. *The Secret Soldier: The Story of Deborah Sampson*. Illustrated by Ann Grifalconi. New York: Four Winds Press, 1975. Grades 3 and up.
At the age of 18 Deborah Sampson donned men's clothing and the name of Robert Shurtliff and joined the Continental Army. She was not discovered until she was hospitalized for an injury.

Meltzer, Milton, editor. *The American Revolutionaries: A History in Their Own Words, 1750-1800*. New York: Thomas Y. Crowell, 1987. Grades 4 and up.
"In letters, diaries, journals, memoirs, interviews, ballads, newspapers, pamphlets and speeches we find the first person evidence of life" from 1750 to 1800. Americans of all ages and backgrounds communicate about their experiences. This is an excellent resource to use when relating war to human beings.

Morris, Richard B. *The American Revolution*. Illustrated by Leonard Everett Fisher. Minneapolis, Minn.: Lerner Publications Company, 1985. Grades 3 and up.
This title provides a brief overview of the war, why it was fought, and its meaning to us today. Illustrations are blue, black, and white.

Quackenbush, Robert. *Pop! Goes the Weasel and Yankee Doodle*. Philadelphia: J. B. Lippincott, 1976. All ages.
With brightly colored illustrations and text Quackenbush contrasts the story of New York during the American Revolution and New York today.

Stein, R. Conrad. *The Story of the Boston Tea Party*. Illustrated by Keith Neely. Chicago: Childrens Press, 1984. Grades 2 and up.
The events leading up to and including the Boston Tea Party are discussed in this short narrative.

Stevens, Bryna. *Deborah Sampson Goes to War*. Illustrated by Florence Hill. Minneapolis, Minn.: Carolrhoda Books, 1984. Grades 1 and up.
This is a very simple version of the story of Deborah Sampson. See McGovern annotation in this section.

Fiction

Anderson, Joan. *1787*. Illustrated by Alexander Farquharson. San Diego: Gulliver Books, 1987. Grades 5 and up.
As aide to James Madison, Jared becomes involved in the framing of the Constitution and the making of history.

Avi. *Captain Grey*. New York: Scholastic Book Services, 1982. Grades 4 and up.
A young boy is captured by pirates during the Revolutionary War.

_____. *The Fighting Ground*. New York: Harper and Row, 1984. Grades 5 and up.
Jonathan is only 13, but he runs away to join the Revolutionary War effort as a soldier. Thoughts of being a hero are forgotten as he faces death and capture.

Bacon, Martha. *Sophia Scrooby Preserved*. Illustrated by David Omar. Boston: Little, Brown and Company, Inc. 1968. Grades 4 and up.
Sophia was the last survivor of an African tribe and daughter of the chieftain. Sold to the Scroobys in New Haven, she begins the adjustment to America until her life is once again disrupted by the Revolutionary War and she is sold to slavers.

Benchley, Nathaniel. *Sam the Minuteman*. Illustrated by Arnold Lobel. New York: Harper and Row, 1969. Grades 1 and up.
In simple text the story of the beginnings of the American Revolution is told by a small boy.

Bourne, Miriam Anne. *Nabby Adam's Diary*. Illustrated by Stephen Gammell. New York: Coward McCann and Geoghegan, 1975. Grades 4 and up.
Bourne uses letters, historical documents, and Nabby's diary to create this fictionalized account of day-to-day life before and during the Revolutionary War.

_____. *Uncle George Washington and Harriot's Guitar*. Illustrated by Elise Primavera. New York: Coward-McCann, Inc., 1983. Grades 3 and up.
Eleven-year-old Harriot was an orphan, relying upon the generosity of her relatives. In correspondence with her famous uncle, she requests a guitar. His response and actions provide another view of Washington.

Boutwell, Edna. *Daughter of Liberty*. Illustrated by Wendy Watson. Cleveland, Ohio: The World Publishing Company, 1967. Grades 4 and up.
Amy is outraged at receiving a doll and being sent to Boston instead of being allowed to fight in Ethan Allen's regiment. The still-existing doll, Polly Sumner, and Amy nevertheless become heroes of the Revolution.

Brady, Esther Wood. *Toliver's Secret*. New York: Crown Publishers, Inc., 1976. Grades 4 and up.
A 10-year-old girl braves enemy lines to deliver a loaf of bread containing a message for the patriots.

Clarke, Mary Stetson. *Petticoat Rebel*. Illustrated by Robert MacLean. New York: Viking Press, 1964. Grades 4 and up.
The schoolmaster left to fight in the war, and Constance is delighted with the opportunity to take his place and promote education for women.

Collier, James Lincoln, and Christopher Collier. *Jump Ship to Freedom*. New York: Dell Publishing Company, Inc., 1981. Grades 4 and up.
Daniel Arabus and his mother are slaves, even though their father, by fighting in the war, earned enough money in notes to buy their freedom. When his father dies, the notes are taken and Daniel steals them back. He is forced to board a ship and must struggle to return to his family and gain their freedom. (Post-Revolutionary War.)

_____. *My Brother Sam Is Dead*. New York: Scholastic Book Services, 1974. Grades 4 and up.
The futility of war is poignantly demonstrated when this family is torn between the opposing forces, and Sam is killed tragically by his compatriots.

_____. *War Comes to Willy Freeman*. New York: Dell Publishing Company, Inc., 1983. Grades 4 and up.
After Willy's father is killed by Redcoats and her mother is taken prisoner, she disguises herself as a boy and sets out in search of her mother.

_____. *Who Is Carrie?* New York: Dell Publishing Company, Inc., 1984. Grades 4 and up.

Carrie, a slave in Sam Fraunces tavern in New York City, is unaware of her heritage. When Daniel Arabus (see *Jump Ship to Freedom*) comes to the tavern, Carrie agrees to help him, learning about her family in the process. (Post-Revolutionary War.)

_____. *The Winter Hero*. New York: Four Winds Press, 1978. Grades 4 and up.

It is 1787, and Justin is part of Shay's Rebellion, a farmers' revolt against the Massachusetts taxes. (Post-Revolutionary War.)

Duncombe, Frances. *Summer of the Burning*. New York: G. P. Putnam's Sons, 1976. Grades 5 and up.

Hannah has survived the death of her mother, the capture of her father by the British, and the burning of their house. She keeps the family together and works for the war effort despite being only 13 years old.

Finlayson, Ann. *Rebecca's War*. Illustrated by Sherry Streeter. New York: Frederick Warne, 1972. Grades 5 and up.

It is the time of the British occupation of Philadelphia in this spirited tale.

Forbes, Esther. *Johnny Tremain*. Illustrated by Lynn Ward. New York: Dell Publishing Company, 1968. Grades 5 and up.

This challenging Newbery book is about a young man's experiences during the Revolutionary War. In contrast to the rural setting of *My Brother Sam Is Dead* (see Collier annotation in this list), this book is set in the city.

Fritz, Jean. *Early Thunder*. Illustrated by Lynn Ward. New York: Coward McCann and Geoghegan, 1967. Grades 4 and up.

Fourteen-year-old Daniel struggles when his dedication to the Tories is challenged. Fritz's story is based on a true confrontation between British troops and the townspeople of Salem.

Haynes, Betsy. *Spies on the Devil's Belt*. Nashville, Tenn.: Thomas Nelson Inc., Publishers, 1974. Grades 4 and up.

In 1779, Johnathan, age 14, signs on with the Continental Army. He runs errands and spies on the British, becoming deeply involved in the war.

Hays, Wilma Pitchford. *Mary's Star: A Tale of Orphans in Virginia in 1781*. Illustrated by Lawrence Beall Smith. New York: Holt, Rinehart and Winston, 1968. Grades 4 and up.

When Mary and her brother learn that their father was killed in the Revolutionary War, they face the challenges of being penniless orphans and the need to keep Mary's colt, Star.

Jenson, Dorothea. *The Riddle of Penncroft Farm*. San Diego: Harcourt Brace Jovanovich, 1989. Grades 4 and up.

Lars Olafson is 12 years old, and he is unhappy when his family moves from Minnesota to a farm near Valley Forge. He soon makes a friend whose stories about the Revolutionary War bring history to life. This mystery intertwines history in an exciting manner.

Lawson, Robert. *Mr. Revere and I*. New York: Dell Publishing Company, Inc., 1953. Grades 4 and up.

Sherry was a horse saved from the glue factory and taken to the house of Paul Revere. She reveals all about Revere and the Sons of Liberty.

Lowrey, Janette. *Six Silver Spoons*. Illustrated by Robert Quackenbush. New York: Harper and Row, 1971. Grades 1 and up.

Two children who are carrying silver spoons made by Paul Revere are helped by a British soldier.

Miers, Earle Schenck. *The Magnificent Mutineers*. Illustrated by W. T. Mars. New York: G. P. Putnam's Sons, 1968. Grades 4 and up.
Told in journal form, the reader learns about Ari Levy, who joins forces against the British and endures the misery of war.

Monjo, F. N. *Indian Summer*. Illustrated by Anita Lobel. New York: Harper and Row, 1968. Grades 1 and up.
A Kentucky woman and her children outwit attacking Indians during Revolutionary War times.

_____. *A Namesake for Nathan*. Illustrated by Eros Keith. New York: Coward McCann and Geoghegan, 1977. Grades 4 and up.
Joanna Hale, the sister of Nathan Hale, tells of their family, which supports the war effort at home while six of the boys are in the Continental Army.

O'Dell, Scott. *Sarah Bishop*. Boston: Houghton Mifflin Company, 1980. Grades 5 and up.
Sarah loses her brother to the war and her father is a prisoner. She is taken prisoner by the British but manages to escape.

Rappaport, Doreen. *The Boston Coffee Party*. Illustrated by Emily Arnold McCully. New York: Harper and Row, 1988. Grades 1 and up.
This easy-to-read book tells the story of the Boston women's revolt against Merchant Thomas, who is overcharging for sugar and coffee.

Schneider, Benjamin. *Winter Patriot*. Philadelphia: Chilton Book Company, 1967. Grades 5 and up.
Seth's father is killed by a Hessian, and Seth joins Grant's troops harrassing the British in New Jersey. A friendship with a deserter teaches him that all Hessians are not like his father's killer.

4
Westward Expansion

Chapter Four
Word List

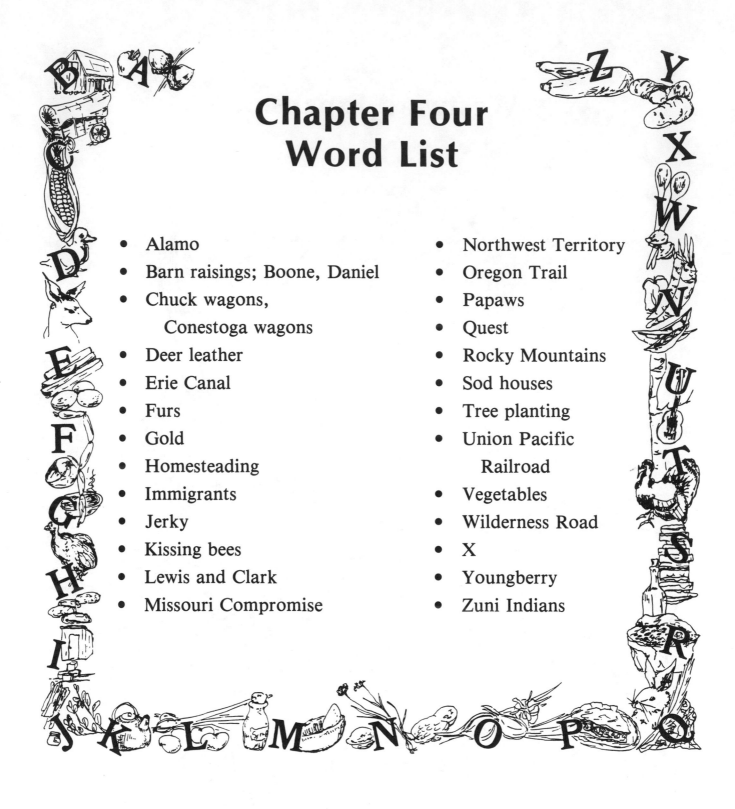

- Alamo
- Barn raisings; Boone, Daniel
- Chuck wagons,
    Conestoga wagons
- Deer leather
- Erie Canal
- Furs
- Gold
- Homesteading
- Immigrants
- Jerky
- Kissing bees
- Lewis and Clark
- Missouri Compromise
- Northwest Territory
- Oregon Trail
- Papaws
- Quest
- Rocky Mountains
- Sod houses
- Tree planting
- Union Pacific
    Railroad
- Vegetables
- Wilderness Road
- X
- Youngberry
- Zuni Indians

SUN-DRIED FRUIT

Ingredients
Fruits, such as raspberries, plums, peaches, etc.

Equipment
Cheesecloth

Steps
1. Wash fruit thoroughly.
2. If fruit has pits, cut fruit in half and remove pits. Slice larger fruit into pieces.
3. Spread the fruit on large cookie sheets.
4. Cover fruit with 1 layer of cheesecloth.
5. Place fruit outside in the sun. Leave it there all day, but take it inside at night.
6. Continue to put it outside each day until it dries and becomes leathery, but not crisp.
7. Store in a tightly covered jar.

Library Link 1: The Cherokee would grow fruits and vegetables during the summer and dry them in the sun or over fires for the winter. Find out how to make Leather Britches Beans.

SOURDOUGH STARTER

Ingredients
½ teaspoon active dry yeast
½ cup very warm water
¾ cups flour
2 cups warm water (110 to 115 degrees)
2½ cups flour

Steps
1. Put first 3 ingredients in a large glass jar.
2. Stir well with a *wooden* spoon.
3. Let mixture sit uncovered for 5 to 6 days or until it bubbles and smells sour. Stir mixture each day.
4. When the mixture is ready, store in the refrigerator.

When you are ready to make biscuits, pancakes, or bread:

1. At least 10 hours before, add rest of the ingredients to the starter.
2. Mix until lumpy.
3. Let the mixture sit out until you are ready to proceed.
4. Remove 1 cup for the next starter and store in refrigerator.
5. Use remainder of starter for your recipe. (Recipes for sourdough biscuits and pancakes follow.)

Library Link 2: Why was a Canadian or Alaskan prospector called a *sourdough*? What were the staples of the prospector's diet?

SOURDOUGH BISCUITS

Ingredients

¾ cup sourdough starter (see preceding recipe) ½ teaspoon salt
1 cup milk 1 tablespoon sugar
3 cups flour ½ teaspoon baking soda

Steps

1. Use warm, bubbly starter. Put it in a large bowl.
2. Add milk to starter.
3. Mix the flour, salt, sugar, and baking soda in another bowl.
4. Stir the flour mixture into the starter mixture.
5. Put dough onto a floured cloth or piece of waxed paper.
6. Roll dough out with a floured rolling pin until it is about ½ inch thick.
7. Cut biscuits out with a 2-inch floured cutter.
8. Place biscuits on a well greased cookie sheet.
9. Cover biscuits with a slightly damp linen towel and put in a warm place to rise.
10. Let biscuits rise for about 30 minutes.
11. Bake biscuits at 375 degrees until slightly brown, about 10 to 15 minutes.

Makes 15.

Library Link 3: Find the origins of sourdough.

SOURDOUGH PANCAKES

Ingredients

1 can evaporated milk 2 tablespoons sugar
¾ cup water 1 teaspoon salt
2 cups flour 2 teaspoons baking soda
1 cup sourdough starter (see page 57) Butter, syrup, or
6 eggs   confectioner's sugar

Steps

1. The night before making pancakes, mix evaporated milk, water, and 2 cups flour into 1 cup sourdough starter.
2. Mix well and cover. Leave out overnight.
3. The next morning heat griddle.
4. Add eggs, sugar, salt, and baking soda to sourdough mixture.
5. Mix well.
6. Grease the griddle lightly.
7. Pour spoonfuls of batter on the griddle.
8. Turn pancakes over when bubbles appear and pancakes are light brown.
9. Serve with butter and syrup or confectioner's sugar.

Makes 35 to 36 4-inch pancakes. To make a smaller batch of pancakes, follow steps 1 and 2. At step 3, separate the mixture into two equal parts. Refrigerate one portion for use another day. Proceed with steps 4 through 9, using 3 eggs, 1 tablespoon sugar, ½ teaspoon salt, and 1 teaspoon baking soda for the pancake batter.

Library Link 4: Why was sourdough not used for many years?

BAKING SODA BISCUITS

Ingredients

2 cups flour
1 teaspoon baking soda
¾ cup sour milk*

1¼ teaspoons salt
2 tablespoons melted shortening
Milk to brush tops of biscuits

Steps

1. Mix flour, salt, and baking soda in a large bowl.
2. Stir in shortening and sour milk until a soft dough forms. Add more milk if necessary.
3. Roll dough out on floured board to 1-inch thickness.
4. Cut out rounds of dough with 2-inch floured cutter.
5. Put biscuits so that sides touch on a greased cookie sheet.
6. Brush tops with plain milk.
7. Bake at 400 degrees for about 15 minutes or until lightly browned.

*To make sour milk, add 1 tablespoons of vinegar or lemon juice to milk and let sit for 10 minutes to curdle.

Makes 10 to 12.

Library Link 5: What was baking soda called in the 1800s?

CORN FRITTERS

Ingredients

1 #2 can corn (20 ounces)
2 eggs
½ cup milk
1 cup flour
1 teaspoon baking powder
1 teaspoon salt
1 teaspoon sugar
Vegetable oil for frying
Optional: syrup, butter, or confectioner's sugar

Steps

1. Strain corn and put it in a large mixing bowl.
2. Add eggs, milk, flour, baking powder, salt, and sugar. Stir until blended.
3. Heat oil in large frying pan or deep fat fryer over medium heat.
4. When oil is hot, drop 1 tablespoon full of batter into the frying pan.
5. Cook 3 minutes and then turn and cook 3 minutes on the other side or until light brown.
6. Drain fritters on paper towels.
7. Serve with butter or maple syrup or roll fritters in confectioner's sugar.

Makes 25 to 30.

Library Link 6: Travelers might use dried corn for recipes like corn soup. How is corn dried?

BAKED BEANS

Ingredients
1½ cups dried beans
Water
½ cup chopped onion
4 tablespoons molasses
3 tablespoons catsup
½ cup brown sugar
1 tablespoon mustard
1 teaspoon salt
¼ pound bacon

Steps
1. Put beans in a large pot and cover with water.
2. Soak beans for 1 hour.
3. Add 3 more cups of water.
4. Boil over low heat for 1 hour.
5. Preheat oven to 250 degrees.
6. Strain beans, but save the water.
7. Put beans in a casserole dish.
8. Add onion, molasses, catsup, brown sugar, mustard, salt and bacon. Stir well.
9. Cover casserole dish and bake 6 to 9 hours or until beans are soft. (Check beans often and add some of the water used to soak the beans if they become dry.)

Serves 4.

Library Link 7: What is the Mexican name for beans? How did pinto beans get their name?

COWBOY PIE

Ingredients
¼ cup shortening
½ cup milk
½ cup flour
1 teaspoon baking powder
¾ teaspoon salt

1 beaten egg
2 tablespoons oil
¾ cup cornmeal
1 tablespoon sugar
2 cans chili

Steps
1. Preheat oven to 400 degrees.
2. Melt shortening in a large saucepan.
3. Remove from heat and stir in egg, milk, and oil.
4. Stir in flour, cornmeal, baking powder, sugar, and salt.
5. Pour chili into an 8-inch square pan.
6. Pour batter over chili.
7. Bake in oven for 15 to 20 minutes.

Serves 4 to 6.

Library Link 8: Find out what a chuck wagon looked like. Draw a picture of one.

TACOS

Ingredients
12 taco shells
1 large can chili without beans
1 onion, chopped fine
2 cups shredded cheese
2 tomatoes, chopped
4 cups shredded lettuce
Bottled picante sauce

Steps
1. Heat oven to 400 degrees.
2. Put taco shells on a cookie sheet.
3. Heat them for 4 minutes.
4. Meanwhile, heat chili in a saucepan until hot.
5. Put chopped onion, cheese, tomatoes, and lettuce in separate bowls.
6. Remove taco shells from oven and fill with chili, onion, cheese, tomatoes, and lettuce.
7. Pour picante sauce over fillings.

Serves 12.

Library Link 9: Research the origin and history of tomatoes.

CRANBERRY JELLY

Ingredients
1 pound cranberries
1¼ cups water
2¼ cups sugar

Steps
1. Wash the cranberries.
2. Put the water in a large saucepan.
3. Add the sugar to the water and boil.
4. Add the berries.
5. Cook 15 to 20 minutes over low heat until berries are soft and mushy.
6. Serve hot or cold.

Serves 6.

Library Link 10: New England Indians called cranberries *sassamanesh*. Where in the United States do cranberries grow? What kind of environment is needed for cranberries?

BIBLIOGRAPHY—WESTWARD EXPANSION

Nonfiction—Series

The Old West. New York: Time-Life Books, varying dates. Grades 6 and up.
Numerous photographs, drawings, maps, and prints are included in these thorough discussions of different aspects of the West. Examples are *The Alaskans, The Forty-niners, The Spanish West, The Pioneers, The Miners, The Ranchers,* and *The Trailblazers*.

Rourke, Arlene, editor. *The Wild West in American History*. Vero Beach, Fla.: Rourke Publications, Inc., varying dates. Grades 3 and up.
These colorful, oversize, easy-to-read books provide a good overview of each subject. Examples are *Railroaders* and *Soldiers*.

Nonfiction—Individual Titles

Aliki. *Johnny Appleseed*. Englewood Cliffs, N.J.: Prentice-Hall, Inc., 1963. All ages.
This picture book has primer-level vocabulary and colorful illustrations.

Bailey, Ralph Edgar. *Wagons Westward! The Story of Alexander Majors*. New York: William Morrow and Company, 1969. Grades 4 and up.
Alexander Majors took his first wagon train to Santa Fe in 1848 and years later had 3,500 wagons on the trails west. This biography gives an excellent overview of the struggles faced by people brave enough to journey west.

Blassingame, Wyatt. *Bent's Fort: Crossroads of the Great West*. Champaign, Ill.: Garrard Publishing Company, 1967. Grades 4 and up.
Bent's Fort served as the marketplace, supply center, and refuge for pioneers of the 1800s. Its story helps readers understand the challenges faced by the settlers.

Blumberg, Rhoda. *The Incredible Journey of Lewis and Clark*. New York: Lothrop Lee and Shepard Company, 1987. Grades 4 and up.
Numerous black-and-white photographs and prints plus extensive text make this oversize book a good first choice for the study of the expedition of Lewis and Clark.

Collins, James L. *Exploring the American West*. New York: Franklin Watts, 1989. Grades 3 and up.
Photographs and lithographs illustrate the stories of Daniel Boone, Lewis and Clark, Robert Stuart and Jed Smith, Joseph Reddeford Walker, and John Charles Fremont.

Davidson, Mary R. *Buffalo Bill*. New York: Dell Publishing Company, Inc., 1962. Grades 2 and up.
This simple chapter book is a biography of Buffalo Bill Cody from his birth in 1846 through his careers on a wagon train, as a rider for the Pony Express, as a scout for the Union Army, as a buffalo hunter for the railroad, and finally, as an entertainer.

DeGering, Etta. *Wilderness Wife: The Story of Rebecca Bryan Boone*. Illustrated by Ursula Koering. New York: Van Rees Press, 1966. Grades 4 and up.
The life of Rebecca Boone provides an often-ignored perspective on pioneer life.

Dines, Glen. *Long Knife: The Story of the Fighting U.S. Cavalry of the 1860 Frontier*. New York: Macmillan Publishing Company, 1961. Grades 3 and up.
Dines's illustrations enhance this description of the challenges faced by the U.S. Cavalry. Quotations, drawings, maps, and even snatches of music provide additional information for the reader.

Freedman, Russell. *Children of the Wild West*. New York: Clarion Books, 1983. Grades 4 and up.
Numerous black-and-white photographs help tell the stories of the children who came west with their families. A chapter is also devoted to American Indian children.

_____. *Cowboys of the Wild West*. New York: Clarion Books, 1985. Grades 4 and up.
After the Civil War the role of the cowboy became increasingly important. Photographs and text tell the story of the cowboy's life on the trail, on the range, and on the ranch.

Fisher, Leonard Everett. *The Alamo*. New York: Holiday House, 1987. Grades 4 and up.
The story of the Alamo is told through text and numerous black-and-white photographs, maps, and drawings.

Flatley, Dennis R. *The Railroads: Opening the West*. New York: Franklin Watts, Inc., 1989. Grades 3 and up.
Flatley describes the development of the railroad from 1800 to the Civil War with text, black-and-white and color photographs, posters, and maps.

Friggens, Myriam. *Tales, Trails and Tommyknockers: Stories from Colorado's Past*. Illustrated by Gene Coulter. Boulder, Colo.: Johnson Publishing Company, 1979. Grades 3 and up.
Line drawings and photographs accompany this collection of stories about people from Colorado's past: Kit Carson, Chief Ouray, Molly Brown, and others.

Grant, Matthew G. *Lewis and Clark: Western Trailblazers*. Illustrated by John Keely and Don Pulver. Mankato, Minn.: Creative Education, 1974. Grades 1 and up.
For the early reader this book provides an overview of the travels of Lewis and Clark. Black-and-white plus color illustrations add interest to their story.

Havighurst, Walter *The First Book of the Oregon Trail*. Illustrated by Helen Borton. New York: Franklin Watts, Inc., 1960. Grades 3 and up.
Beginning with the Lewis and Clark Expedition, continuing with a wagon train, and ending with the advent of train travel, Havighurst provides an overview of the settling of the West.

_____. *The First Book of the Pioneers: Northwest Territory*. Illustrated by Harve Stein. New York: Franklin Watts, Inc., 1959. Grades 4 and up.
Through the family of Jason Stone, readers learn about the challenges of moving and settling in the West in the early 1800s.

Jakes, John. *Susanna of the Alamo: A True Story*. Illustrated by Paul Bacon. San Diego: Harcourt Brace Jovanovich, 1986. Grades 2 and up.
When General Santa Ana conquered the Alamo, he spared Susanna Dickinson's life, intending that her story would warn off the rebels. Instead her courage inspired General Sam Houston's men to later victory.

Keating, Bern. *Famous American Explorers*. Illustrated by Lorence Bjorklund. Chicago: Rand McNally and Company, 1972. Grades 4 and up.
Beginning with the Vikings, Keating traces the exploration of America through the westward expansion. This oversize book includes line drawings in black and white and color.

Laycock, George, and Ellen Laycock. *How the Settlers Lived*. Illustrated by Alexander Farquharson. New York: David McKay Company, Inc., 1980. Grades 4 and up.
    The journey west was just the beginning of the challenges faced by the settlers. The Laycocks describe the homes, farming, hunting, clothing, habits, and recreation of the pioneers.

May, Robin. *An American Pioneer Family*. Illustrated by Mark Bergin. Vero Beach, Fla.: Rourke Enterprises, Inc., 1985. Grades 2 and up.
    Simple text and colorful pictures tell the story of pioneer life from the journey through settling in a home and everyday life.

McCall, Edith. *Cowboys and Cattle Drives*. Illustrated by Carol Rogers. Chicago: Childrens Press, 1980. Grades 3 and up.
    The stories of men who helped settle the West in the 1800s are told: Charlie Goodnight, James Cook, Tom Smith, and Will Rogers.

_____. *Cumberland Gap*. Illustrated by Carol Rogers. Chicago: Childrens Press, 1980. Grades 3 and up.
    McCall tells the stories of Thomas Batts, Gabe Arthur, Thomas Walker, Daniel Boone, and others who explored the West.

_____. *Forts in the Wilderness*. Illustrated by Darrell Wiskur. Chicago: Childrens Press, 1980. Grades 3 and up.
    The exploration of the Midwest is told through the stories of LaSalle and Pontiac.

_____. *Heroes of the Western Outposts*. Illustrated by William Tanis. Chicago: Childrens Press, 1980. Grades 3 and up.
    The early 1800s were the time of establishing forts in the west. Stories are told of John Colter, Jim Bridger, Wild Bill Hickok, and others.

_____. *Hunters Blaze the Trails*. Illustrated by Carol Rogers. Chicago: Childrens Press, 1980. Grades 3 and up.
    More stories of heroes of the early 1800s are told: Davy Crockett, Kit Carson, Bill Cody, and others.

_____. *Wagons Over the Mountains*. Illustrated by Carol Rogers. Chicago: Childrens Press, 1961. Grades 3 and up.
    Seven stories of pioneer travels westward are told by McCall. The stories are based on true accounts of settlers.

Perl, Lila. *Hunter's Stew and Hangtown Fry: What Pioneer America Ate and Why*. Illustrated by Richard Cuffari. New York: Seabury Press, 1977. Grades 4 and up.
    Perl explores the role of food throughout the westward movement. She includes the adaptations of food made necessary by the conditions as well as the contributions of immigrant groups.

Phelan, Mary Kay. *Waterway West: The Story of the Erie Canal*. Illustrated by David Frampton. New York: Thomas Y. Crowell, 1977. Grades 4 and up.
    The Erie Canal, America's first major waterway, opened in 1825, linking the Hudson River and the Great Lakes. Using journals and letters, Phelan describes the development of the canal.

Place, Marian T. *The First Book of the Santa Fe Trail*. Illustrated by Paul Frame. New York: Franklin Watts, Inc., 1966. Grades 4 and up.
    The story of the Santa Fe Trail began in 1806 when Congress sent Lieutenant Zebulon M. Pike to explore the southern boundary of the Louisiana Purchase. When he stumbled into Spanish territory he was arrested and taken to Santa Fe.

Quackenbush, Robert. *Quit Pulling My Leg: A Story of Davy Crockett*. New York: Prentice-Hall, Inc., 1987. Grades 3 and up.
This humorous biography of Davy Crockett examines the fact and fantasy surrounding his life.

Rich, Louis Dickinson. *The First Book of the Fur Trade*. Illustrated by Claudine Nankivel. New York: Franklin Watts, Inc., 1965. Grades 4 and up.
The story of the settling of the West is described through the lives of the French, English, and American fur traders and mountain men, such as Jim Bridger.

Rieupeyrout, Jean-Louis. *The American West*. Illustrated by Jose Mari Miralles. Morristown, N.J.: Silver Burdett, 1982. Grades 3 and up.
The 17 states west of the Missouri are discussed with many color pictures, maps, and drawings.

Rounds, Glen. *The Cowboy Trade*. New York: Holiday House, 1972. Grades 3 and up.
Rounds covers the role of the cowboy from his work day to his portrayal in television, film, and fiction. Rounds's humorous style and line drawings provide an enjoyable book.

_____. *The Prairie Schooners*. New York: Holiday House, 1968. Grades 3 and up.
Rounds begins the journey west at Independence, Missouri, providing a lively and intriguing description of the next two thousand miles.

Skold, Betty Westrom. *Sacagawea: The Story of an American Indian*. Minneapolis, Minn.: Dillon Press, Inc., 1978. Grades 5 and up.
Sacagawea (Sacajawea) is traded to Toussaint Charbonneau, a French-Canadian fur trader, by a tribe that had held her hostage. He is hired as the interpreter for the Lewis and Clark expedition, and she proves to be an invaluable aide.

Stein, R. Conrad. *The Lewis and Clark Expedition*. Illustrated by Lou Aronson. Chicago: Childrens Press, 1978. Grades 3 and up.
The reader travels along as Lewis and Clark, with 30 men, set off down the Missouri River. This book provides a good introduction to the exploration of the western half of the country.

Surge, Frank. *Western Lawmen*. Minneapolis, Minn.: Lerner Publications Company, 1969. Grades 3 and up.
Surge provides brief biographies of many western lawmen, including Wild Bill Hickok, Tom Smith, Bat Masterson, Wyatt Earp, and Judge Roy Bean.

_____. *Western Outlaws*. Minneapolis, Minn.: Lerner Publications Company, 1969. Grades 3 and up.
Posters and photographs help illustrate the stories of Jesse James, Billy the Kid, Black Bart, Sam Bass, Belle Starr, the Daltons, and other notorious outlaws.

Syme, Ronald. *John Charles Fremont: The Last American Explorer*. Illustrated by Richard Cuffari. New York: William Morrow and Company, 1974. Grades 4 and up.
Based on diaries and letters, Syme describes Fremont's five expeditions and his later problems.

Wolf, Bernard. *Cowboy*. New York: William Morrow and Company, 1985. Grades 4 and up.
Though about today's cowboys, this account of a Montana cattle ranch provides fascinating information about the cowboy's work.

Fiction

Altsheler, Joseph A. *Kentucky Frontiermen*. Illustrated by Todd Doney. Nashville, Tenn.: Voyageur
   Publishing Inc., 1988. Grades 4 and up.
   Originally published in 1906 as *The Young Trailers*, this revised and updated version tells of the
challenges of settling in Kentucky.

Anderson, Joan. *Joshua's Westward Journal*. Photographs by George Ancona. New York: William
   Morrow and Company, 1987. Grades 1 and up.
   Photographed at the Living History Farms in Des Moines, Iowa, this is the story of a family's move
west in a Conestoga wagon.

Bohner, Charles. *Bold Journey: West with Lewis and Clark*. Boston: Houghton Mifflin Company, 1985.
   Grades 4 and up.
   Private Hugh McNeal's name is listed as a member of the Lewis and Clark expedition. This is an
imaginary account of his adventure on that journey.

Brenner, Barbara. *Wagon Wheels*. Illustrated by Don Bolognese. New York: Harper and Row, 1978.
   Grades 1 and up.
   It is the 1870s, and a black family is traveling from Kentucky to Kansas. The three young boys must
survive without their father while he moves ahead.

Brown, Irene Bennett. *Before the Lark*. New York: Atheneum, 1982. Grades 5 and up.
   Jocey is disfigured by a harelip and is living with her grandmother after her father abandons her. She
looks forward to their move to a deserted farm.

Bulla, Clyde Robert. *Riding the Pony Express*. Illustrated by Grace Paull. New York: Thomas Y. Crowell,
   1948. Grades 2 and up.
   Simple text and dialogue tell the story of a young boy's adventures at a Pony Express way station and
his friendship with an Indian boy.

Calvert, Patricia. *The Snowbird*. New York: Charles Scribner's Sons, 1980. Grades 5 and up.
   Orphans Willanna and TJ must go to the Dakota Territory to live with their aunt and uncle. A mare,
named Snowbird by Willanna, helps her find peace with her lot.

Clark, Ann Nolan. *All This Wild Land*. New York: Viking Press, 1976. Grades 5 and up.
   Maiju and her family travel from Finland to Minnesota in 1876. The challenges of the first year include
tragedy, but the support of family and friends helps her develop courage.

Coatsworth, Elizabeth. *The Sod House*. New York: Macmillan Publishing Company, 1954. Grades 2 and
   up.
   In simple text, the story is told of the Traubel family, who left Boston for Kansas, searching for a better
way of life.

Coerr, Eleanor. *The Josefina Story Quilt*. Illustrated by Bruce Degen. New York: Harper and Row,
   1986. All ages.
   Josefina the hen was a nuisance on the Faith family's trip west until her squawking saves them from
robbers.

Collier, James Lincoln, and Christopher Collier. *The Bloody Country*. New York: Four Winds Press, 1976. Grades 4 and up.

Ben and his family struggle with other settlers to keep their lands and homes in Pennsylvania during the late 1700s.

Colver, Anne. *Bread-and-Butter Journey*. New York: Holt, Rinehart and Winston, 1970. Grades 2 and up.

Following *Bread-and-Butter Indian* (see Colver annotation, chapter 1), Barbara, her mother, and another family set off for western Pennsylvania with only her brother and another young boy as guides. This is based on the history of Colver's husband's family.

Flory, Jane. *The Golden Venture*. Boston: Houghton Mifflin Company, 1967. Grades 4 and up.

Minne stows away in a wagon to go with her father to the gold fields in San Francisco. There she begins a business with two unusual ladies.

Frazier, Neta Lohnes. *Stout-Hearted Seven: The True Adventure of the Sager Children Orphaned on the Oregon Trail in 1844*. New York: Harcourt Brace Jovanovich, 1973. Grades 5 and up.

Losing their parents in 1844, the seven children are adopted by the Whitmans. In 1847 the family is devastated when Cayuse Indians kill the Whitmans and two of the children. See also Lampman's *Cayuse Courage* (annotated in chapter 1) for a companion piece based on the Whitman Massacre.

Fritz, Jean. *The Cabin Faced West*. Illustrated by Feodor Rojankovsky. New York: Coward-McCann, Inc., 1958. Grades 3 and up.

Ann learns of the hardships and pleasures of life in a cabin in the western Pennsylvania wilderness. This is based on the life of Fritz's great-great-grandmother.

Harvey, Brett. *Cassie's Journey: Going West in the 1860s*. Illustrated by Deborah Kogan Ray. New York: Holiday House, 1988. Grades 1 and up.

Cassie's family left Illinois for California, and Cassie describes the challenges of their journey.

Henry, Joanne Landers. *Log Cabin in the Woods: A True Story about a Pioneer Boy*. Illustrated by Joyce Audy Zarins. New York: Macmillan Publishing Company, 1988. All ages.

Life was challenging, yet never dull, for a twelve-year-old boy growing up in the Indiana woods. This is a retelling of the true story of Oliver Johnson's early years, as originally told to his grandson, Howard Johnson.

Hunt, Irene. *Trail of Apple Blossoms*. Chicago: Follett Publishing Company, 1968. Grades 3 and up.

The Bryants move from Boston to the Midwest and are befriended by Johnny Appleseed.

Kherdian, David. *Jim Bridger: The Story of a Mountain Man*. New York: Greenwillow Books, 1987. Grades 4 and up.

In 1822 Jim Bridger signs up with General Ashley to explore the Missouri River. Jim travels, lives with Crow Indians, falls in love with an Indian girl, and at age twenty discovers the Great Salt Lake.

Lampman, Evelyn Sibley. *Wheels West*. Garden City, N.Y.: Doubleday and Company, Inc., 1969. Grades 5 and up.

This story of the covered wagon journey to Oregon is based on the life of Tabitha Brown.

————. *White Captives*. New York: Atheneum, 1975. Grades 5 and up.

In retaliation for the massacre of some of their women and children, Indians kill all but two girls from a family headed to the Southwest. Their five years in captivity during the 1850s are presented with sympathy for both sides.

Levitin, Sonia. *The No-Return Trail*. New York: Harcourt Brace Jovanovich, 1978. Grades 5 and up.

Nancy is seventeen, traveling with her husband and baby from Missouri to California. This is a fictionalized account of the first woman to make the journey overland.

Moeri, Louise. *Save Queen of Sheba*. New York: Avon Books, 1981. Grades 5 and up.

During an Indian attack, King David and Queen of Sheba are separated from their family. Everyone else is dead, and David must convince his sister to face hardships bravely in their journey.

Sanders, Scott Russell. *Aurora Means Dawn*. Illustrated by Jill Kastner. New York: Bradbury Press, 1989. All ages.

Lovely watercolors enhance this touching story of a family's move to Ohio in the 1800s. Expecting to arrive at a town, not a piece of land, they are nevertheless undaunted and meet the challenge of settling there.

Sandin, Joan. *The Long Way Westward*. New York: Harper and Row, 1989. Grades 1 and up.

This easy-to-read book tells the story of a family that left Sweden and moved from New York to Minnesota.

Shaffer, Ann. *The Camel Express*. Illustrated by Robin Cole. Minneapolis, Minn.: Dillon Press, Inc., 1989. Grades 3 and up.

When the Pony Express rider is hurt, Grandpa and Mary Claire ride a camel to the next post.

Shub, Elizabeth. *The White Stallion*. Illustrated by Rachel Isadora. New York: Greenwillow Books, 1982. Grades 1 and up.

Based on a true account, this is the story of a young girl who is carried away by an old mare from a wagon train to join a herd of wild horses. A white stallion saves her.

Steele, William O. *The Buffalo Knife*. Illustrated by Paul Galdone. Boston: Harcourt Brace Jovanovich, 1952. Grades 4 and up.

A nine-year-old boy takes an exciting, thousand-mile journey on a flatboat.

Turner, Ann. *Dakota Dugout*. New York: Macmillan Publishing Company, 1985. Grades 1 and up.

Life in a sod house is described, including the killing winter, the summer drought, and the unending isolation. Finally the family's existence improves, but the early years are remembered fondly.

_____. *Grasshopper Summer*. New York: Macmillan Publishing Company, 1989. Grades 4 and up.

The Civil War is over and Sem's father wants to make a new life in the Dakota Territory. The journey is difficult, the sod house is confining, but the worst is yet to come. Grasshoppers devour the family's long-awaited first harvest.

Yates, Elizabeth. *Carolina's Courage*. New York: G. P. Putnam's Sons, 1964. Grades 3 and up.

Carolina, her family, and her china doll leave New Hampshire to settle in the West in the 1800s.

5
The Civil War

Chapter Five
Word List

- Appomattox
- Blockade runners
- Confederates, Carpetbaggers
- Dred Scott decision
- Exposure
- Food processing
- Gettysburg; Grant, Ulysses S.
- Homestead Act
- Icehouse
- Juice
- Kearney, General Philip
- Little Round Top
- Mules
- Naval warfare
- Oil
- Profiteers
- Quantrill, William C.
- Railroads
- Sherman, William T.
- Transportation
- Underground Railroad
- Vegetable preservation
- Wagons
- X
- Yankee
- Zoaves

A Soldier's Daily Camp Ration:
   12 ounces of pork or bacon or 20 ounces salted or fresh beef
   22 ounces soft bread or flour or 16 ounces hard bread or 20 ounces corn meal

With every hundred such rations, there should be:
   1 peck of beans or peas
   10 pounds of rice or hominy
   10 pounds of green coffee or 8 pounds of roasted and ground coffee or 1 and ½ pounds of tea
   15 pounds of sugar
   20 ounces of candles
   4 pounds of soap
   2 quarts of salt
   4 quarts of vinegar
   4 ounces pepper
   ½ bushel potatoes
   1 quart molasses

Marching Ration:
   1 pound hard bread
   ¾ pound salt pork or 1¼ pound fresh meat
   Sugar
   Coffee
   Salt

Source: Billings, John D. *Hardtack and Coffee: The Unwritten Story of Army Life*. Illustrated by Charles W. Reed. Boston: George M. Smith and Company, 1887.

BUTTERMILK PANCAKES

Ingredients

1 cup flour	1 egg
2 teaspoons sugar	2 tablespoons melted butter
½ teaspoon salt	1 cup buttermilk or sour milk*
½ teaspoon baking powder	1 tablespoon shortening
½ teaspoon baking soda	Butter and maple syrup

Steps

1. Mix flour, sugar, salt, baking powder, and baking soda in a large bowl.
2. Beat egg in a small bowl. Add the butter and milk. Mix well.
3. Pour liquid mixture into dry mixture. Stir only long enough to wet the dry ingedients. Do not overbeat.
4. Heat a griddle over medium heat, or heat electric griddle to medium setting.
5. Melt tablespoon of shortening on griddle.
6. Drop batter onto hot griddle.
7. When holes or bubbles appear evenly on the top of each pancake, turn it over.
8. Cook until brown on both sides.
9. Serve hot with butter and maple syrup.

*To make sour milk, add 1 tablespoon vinegar or lemon juice to milk and let stand for 10 minutes to curdle.

Makes 10 to 12 pancakes.

Library Link 1: Who was Gail Borden? What important role did he play during the Civil War?

DOUGH NUTS

Ingredients

4 tablespoons butter	1 teaspoon baking powder
½ cup sugar	2½ cups flour
2 eggs	Oil for frying
¼ teaspoon salt	Sugar for sprinkling over
½ teaspoon cinnamon	cooked dough nuts

Steps

1. Cream butter and sugar together.
2. Beat in eggs.
3. Stir in salt, cinnamon, and baking powder.
4. Stir in enough of the flour to form a stiff dough, then turn dough out onto table and knead in the rest of the flour.
5. Heat about 3 inches of oil in a heavy pan.
6. Roll dough into balls about 1½ inches wide.
7. Drop balls into hot fat and cook until brown on all sides.
8. Remove balls from hot fat with a slotted spoon and drain on paper towels.
9. Sprinkle sugar over each dough nut.

Makes 8 to 12.

Library Link 2: These dough nuts did not have holes. When were holes added to what we now call "doughnuts" (spelled closed up)?

FRIED POTATOES

Ingredients
Potatoes
Butter for frying
Salt, to taste

Steps
1. Peel potatoes.
2. Cut potatoes into thin slices.
3. Melt butter in frying pan over medium heat.
4. Add potato slices to pan and fry until brown on both sides.
5. Add salt to taste.

Library Link 3: Where did potatoes originate? How did they get to North America?

HARDTACK

Ingredients
3 cups flour
2 teaspoons salt
1 cup water

Steps
1. In a large bowl, mix flour and salt.
2. Add water and stir or work with hands to blend.
3. Knead dough, adding more flour if mixture becomes sticky. Turn out onto a floured board.
4. Roll the dough into a rectangle ½ inch thick.
5. Using a sharp knife, cut the dough into 3-inch squares.
6. Using a large, clean nail, poke 16 holes through each square.
7. Bake at 375 degrees for 25 minutes or until brown.
8. Store in an airtight container.

Makes 12.

Library Link 4: Hardtack was a staple of the Civil War soldier. Often it was infested with weevils. What are weevils?

BEATEN BISCUITS

Ingredients
4 cups flour
1¼ teaspoons salt
2 teaspoons sugar
4 tablespoons lard or 5 tablespoons softened margarine
½ cup cold milk
½ cup cold water
Melted butter

Steps
1. Mix flour, salt, and sugar well in a large bowl.
2. Work lard into the dry ingredients with a pastry blender or with hands.
3. Slowly add the milk and water, stirring constantly until it forms a soft dough. Use your hands, but do not overmix.
4. Place a clean linen towel on the table and sprinkle with flour.
5. Place the dough on the towel and beat with a wooden mallet or rolling pin until it is flattened.
6. Fold the sides up to the center and beat until flattened again.
7. Continue beating and folding for 20 minutes.
8. During the last beating, beat to about 1 inch high and cut out with round cutters dipped in flour.
9. Poke top of biscuits with a fork and brush with melted butter.
10. Bake at 350 degrees for 25 minutes or until browned.

Makes 10.

Library Link 5: What effect did the passing of the Homestead Act have on farming?

CHICKEN PIE

Ingredients

Crust
⅔ cup shortening
2 cups flour
½ teaspoon salt
¼ cup cold water

Filling
3 cups cooked chicken, cut into bite-size pieces
2 slices raw bacon
⅓ cup flour
2 eggs
1 cup chicken broth
Salt and pepper, to taste

Steps
1. Work shortening into flour and salt with a pastry blender or hands.
2. Sprinkle with cold water and toss with a fork until dough forms a ball. Do not add more water than necessary and do not overmix.
3. Divide dough into 2 equal parts.
4. Roll 1 part into a 12-inch circle.
5. Line a 9-inch pie pan with the dough. Trim the edge to 1 inch wider than the pan.
6. Sprinkle the cooked chicken evenly over the bottom of the crust.
7. Cut bacon into small pieces and sprinkle over the chicken.
8. Sprinkle ⅓ cup of flour over chicken and bacon.
9. Beat eggs in a small bowl.
10. Beat chicken broth into eggs.
11. Pour liquid mixture over the chicken mixture.
12. Salt and pepper to taste.
13. Roll second part of dough into a 12-inch circle.
14. Cover pie with dough, folding under and sealing edges.
15. Use a knife to cut 3 slashes about 1 inch long in the top crust.
16. Bake at 375 degrees for 45 minutes or until browned and bubbly.

Makes 1 9-inch pie.

Library Link 6: Research the contrast between food production in the North and in the South during the Civil War.

SPONGE CAKE

Ingredients
6 eggs, separated
¼ teaspoon salt
2 cups sugar
2¼ cups flour

Steps
1. Beat egg whites until stiff.
2. Beat in salt.
3. Beat egg yolks in a separate bowl.
4. Slowly add sugar to egg yolks while beating.
5. Continue beating until thick and lemon colored.
6. Gently fold yolk mixture into egg whites.
7. Gently fold in flour.
8. Grease and flour a 9-inch tube pan.
9. Carefully spoon batter into pan.
10. Bake at 375 degrees for 1 hour or until done.

Makes 1 cake.

Library Link 7:   What effect did Sherman's march to the sea have on the food supplies of the South?

GINGERBREAD

Ingredients
½ cup softened butter or margarine
½ cup sugar
¾ cup molasses
2 eggs
1 tablespoon ginger
1½ teaspoons cinnamon
2½ teaspoons baking soda
¾ cup boiling water
2¾ cups flour

Steps
1. Cream butter or margarine.
2. Stir sugar, molasses, and eggs into butter.
3. Stir in ginger, cinnamon, and baking soda.
4. Stir in half of the water, then half of the flour.
5. Stir in the rest of the water, then the rest of the flour.
6. Grease a 9 inch by 13 inch baking pan.
7. Pour batter into the pan and bake at 350 degrees for 25 minutes or until center springs back when touched lightly.

Serves 16.

Library Link 8:   Where did ginger come from?

APPLEADE

Ingredients
2 large apples
1 quart water
Sugar to taste

Steps
1. Core and cut apples into slices. Do not peel. Place in a pan.
2. Boil the water.
3. Pour boiling water over apple slices.
4. Let sit for 30 minutes.
5. Strain well.
6. Sweeten to taste.
7. Chill.

Serves 6.

Library Link 9: Approximately how much did a barrel of apple cider cost during the Civil War?

HOT CHOCOLATE

Ingredients
1½ cups water
1 ounce unsweetened chocolate
¼ cup sugar
2¼ cups milk

Steps
1. Put water in a medium saucepan and bring to a boil over medium high heat.
2. Turn heat down to medium low and add chocolate. Stir until chocolate melts.
3. Add sugar and stir until dissolved.
4. Stir in milk.
5. Serve hot.

Serves 4.

Library Link 10: How was the cacao bean prepared for a chocolate drink?

BARLEY WATER

Ingredients
½ cup barley
3 pints water
Peel of 1 lemon
Sugar to taste

Steps
1. Put barley, water, and lemon peel in a saucepan.
2. Simmer for 30 to 45 minutes.
3. Add sugar to taste.
4. Strain and drink while hot.

Serves 6.

Library Link 11: The Civil War soldiers loved coffee, but often substituted grains for coffee. What else did they use to make coffee substitutes?

BIBLIOGRAPHY—THE CIVIL WAR

Nonfiction

Coffey, Vincent J. *The Battle of Gettysburg*. Morristown, N.J.: Silver Burdett, 1985. Grades 4 and up.
    Photographs and maps illustrate the text that describes the events leading up to, during, and following the battle at Gettysburg.

d'Aulaire, Ingri, and Edgar d'Aulaire. *Abraham Lincoln*. Garden City, N.Y.: Doubleday and Company, Inc., 1957. Grades 2 and up.
    Lincoln's youth is emphasized in this colorful, oversize biography.

Davis, Burke. *Runaway Balloon: The Last Flight of Confederate Air Force One*. Illustrated by Salvatore Murdocca. New York: Coward McCann and Geoghegan, 1976. Grades 3 and up.
    The Yankees were spying on the Confederates from a hot air balloon, motivating the Confederates to create their own balloon. Reluctantly, Lieutenant Bryan flew in the balloon, only to be shot at. His second voyage ended in his losing his clothing and returning to earth naked. The line drawings add interest to this amusing war story.

Freedman, Russell. *Lincoln: A Photobiography*. New York: Scholastic Book Services, 1987. Grades 4 and up.
    Photographs, posters, portraits, and text provide an enlightening biography of Lincoln. This is a Newbery Medal book.

Freeman, Fred. *Duel of the Ironclads*. New York: Time-Life Books, 1969. Grades 3 and up.
    Freeman's maps, charts, and illustrations tell the story of the battle between the *Merrimack* and the *Monitor*. Though the confrontation was considered a standoff, it affected the future of naval warfare.

Horgan, Paul. *Citizen of New Salem*. Illustrated by Douglas Gorsline. New York: Farrar, Straus and Cudahy, 1961. Grades 5 and up.
Lincoln's years in New Salem, Illinois, from age twenty-one to twenty-eight, are described in this acclaimed biography. The story and line drawings provide the reader with intriguing insights into frontier times.

Jordan, Robert Paul. *The Civil War*. Washington, D.C.: National Geographic Society, 1969. Grades 4 and up.
An abundance of colorful photographs, maps, charts, and illustrations give the reader a broad understanding of the agonies of the Civil War. The text provides the research student with a wealth of material.

Katz, William Loren. *An Album of the Civil War*. New York: Franklin Watts, Inc., 1974. Grades 3 and up.
The liberal use of original prints and photographs makes this album an intriguing resource. Text is provided primarily to explain the photographs, yet it provides a wealth of background information about the war.

Kent, Zachary. *John Brown's Raid on Harpers Ferry*. Chicago: Childrens Press, 1988. Grades 3 and up.
John Brown intended to provide slaves with weapons, and he led a raid on the arsenal at Harpers Ferry. The thirty-six-hour raid resulted in the loss of seventeen lives. Photographs illustrate his raid, capture, and execution.

_____. *The Story of the Battle of Bull Run*. Illustrated by David J. Catrow III. Chicago: Childrens Press, 1986. Grades 3 and up.
Black, white, and brown line drawings illustrate the story of this famous battle. The contrast between the sightseeing crowds and the reality of 900 dead and thousands injured is clearly described.

_____. *The Story of Ford's Theater and the Death of Lincoln*. Chicago: Childrens Press, 1987. Grades 3 and up.
Photographs of the theater, historical paintings, and the room where Lincoln died enhance this recounting of the events surrounding Lincoln's assassination.

_____. *The Story of Sherman's March to the Sea*. Illustrated by Ralph Canaday. Chicago: Childrens Press, 1987. Grades 3 and up.
General William Tecumseh Sherman led his soldiers on a 300-mile march of destruction, demonstrating the strength of the Union Army to the Southerners.

_____. *The Story of the Surrender at Appomattox Court House*. Chicago: Childrens Press, 1987. Grades 3 and up.
The surrender of General Lee at Appomattox is described through text and reproductions of a variety of prints. The humane treatment of the Confederates and the courage of all the soldiers is described with dignity.

Latham, Frank B. *Lincoln and the Emancipation Proclamation, January 1, 1863: The Document that Turned the Civil War into a Fight for Freedom*. New York: Franklin Watts, Inc., 1969. Grades 4 and up.
The Emancipation Proclamation, the Lincoln-Douglas debates, and the events leading up to the beginning of the Civil War are illustrated through the use of prints, posters, and text.

Levenson, Dorothy. *The First Book of the Civil War*. New York: Franklin Watts, Inc., 1968. Grades 4 and up.

Original Civil War drawings and photographs provide the reader with an intimate look at the horrors of the Civil War. The text provides a good overview of the war, and the index assists the beginning research student.

Monjo, F. N. *Me and Willie and Pa: The Story of Abraham Lincoln and His Son Tad*. Illustrated by Douglas Gorsline. New York: Simon and Schuster, 1973. Grades 4 and up.

Tad Lincoln tells the story of his life with his brother, Willie, and his father, Abraham Lincoln. Tad's perspective and the numerous portraits bring this era alive.

Richards, Kenneth. *The Story of the Gettysburg Address*. Illustrated by Tom Dunnington. Chicago: Childrens Press, 1969. Grades 3 and up.

The devastation at the Battle of Gettysburg was extensive. Lincoln prepared only 268 words for his memorable speech at the Soldier's National Cemetery. Black, white, and tan drawings collaborate with the text to tell the story of Lincoln's famous speech.

Fiction

Archer, Myrth. *The Young Boys Gone*. New York: Walker and Company, 1978. Grades 5 and up.

A family struggles to survive in the Ozark wilderness during the Civil War. Thad tries to reconcile the war, slavery, and the environment.

Beatty, Patricia. *Be Ever Hopeful, Hannalee*. New York: Morrow Junior Books, 1988. Grades 5 and up.

The Civil War is finally over, and instead of returning home to stay, Hannalee must join her brother in Atlanta, where she faces hard work and danger. See *Turn Homeward, Hannalee*, below.

_____. *Charley Skedaddle*. New York: Morrow Junior Books, 1987. Grades 4 and up.

Charley's brother is killed, and Charley enlists in the Union Army as a drummer boy. When he experiences his first battle he flees to the mountains, where he resolves his feelings of cowardice.

_____. *A Long Way to Whiskey Creek*. New York: Morrow Junior Books, 1971. Grades 4 and up.

Two boys grapple with the hostility between Northern and Southern supporters.

_____. *Turn Homeward, Hannalee*. New York: William Morrow and Company, 1984. Grades 5 and up.

Hannalee is a twelve-year-old textile-mill hand when she is forced from her Georgia home to work in the Yankee mills during the Civil War. See *Be Ever Hopeful, Hannalee*, above.

Burchard, Peter. *The Deserter: A Spy Story of the Civil War*. New York: Coward McCann and Geoghegan, 1973. Grades 4 and up.

This is the story of Levi Blair, who chose to be a deserter in order to spy. Based in part on fact.

_____. *Jed*. New York: Coward McCann and Geoghegan, 1960. Grades 5 and up.

Sixteen-year-old Jed fights at Shiloh on the Yankee side, but befriends an injured young Confederate boy.

_____. *North by Night*. New York: Coward McCann and Geoghegan, 1962. Grades 4 and up.

Two Yankee soldiers escape from a Confederate prison.

Clapp, Patricia. *The Tamarack Tree*. New York: Lothrop Lee and Shepard Company, 1986. Grades 5 and up.

As a thirteen-year-old orphan, Rosemary left England and came to Vicksburg. The conflicts of the Civil War are presented through her unbiased point of view, but the siege of Vicksburg becomes a test of her courage.

Crane, Stephen. *Red Badge of Courage*. Illustrated by Herschel Levit. New York: Macmillan Publishing Company, 1962. Grades 5 and up.

The horror of war is experienced in this moving novel about Henry Fleming, a young farm boy who enlists to fight in the Union Army.

Gauch, Patricia Lee. *Thunder at Gettysburg*. Illustrated by Stephen Gammell. New York: Coward McCann and Geoghegan, 1975. Grades 2 and up.

The Battle of Gettysburg promises to provide great entertainment, but Tillie quickly discovers just how devastating war can be.

Hall, Anna Gertrude. *Cyrus Holt and the Civil War*. Illustrated by Dorothy Bayley Morse. New York: Viking Press, 1964. Grades 5 and up.

The Civil War begins when Cyrus is nine. The impact of the war on his family and friends is seen through Cyrus's eyes.

Hamilton, Virginia. *Anthony Burns: The Defeat and Triumph of a Fugitive Slave*. New York: Alfred A. Knopf, Inc., 1988. Grades 6 and up.

Anthony Burns, an escaped slave from Virginia, was captured in Boston, tried, and returned to slavery. His biography is a poignant reminder of the challenges faced by slaves.

Hansen, Joyce. *Out from This Place*. New York: Walker and Company, 1988. Grades 4 and up.

A fourteen-year-old black girl searches for a fellow ex-slave during the turbulent period after the Civil War.

_____. *Which Way to Freedom*. New York: Walker and Company, 1986. Grades 4 and up.

Obi is a slave who escapes to fight in a black Union regiment. This important book addresses the black contributions to the war effort.

Haynes, Betty. *Cowslip*. Nashville, Tenn.: Thomas Nelson Inc., Publishers, 1973. Grades 4 and up.

The Civil War had begun when Cowslip was on the auction block. After being sold she is profoundly affected by her new friends, who strive for freedom.

Hiser, Berniece T. *The Adventure of Charlie and His Wheat-Straw Hat: A Memorat*. Illustrated by Mary Szilagyi. New York: Dodd, Mead and Company, 1989. All ages.

Charlie's dad had left to fight in the Civil War, leaving Charlie with the family in their Appalachian mountain home. When soldiers come to steal Squire McIntosh's animals, Charlie's treasured straw hat is almost lost. Based on a true incident.

Hunt, Irene. *Across Five Aprils*. New York: Berkley Books, 1986. Grades 5 and up.

Jethro's life is disrupted when he must take over the work of the farm while the men fight in the Civil War. The historical details of this rich novel make it ideal for the study of the Civil War.

Hurmence, Belinda. *Tancy*. New York: Clarion Books, 1984. Grades 4 and up.

    The Civil War is over, and Tancy leaves the plantation in search of her mother, Lulu, during the difficult time of the Reconstruction period.

Keith, Harold. *Rifles for Watie*. New York: Thomas Y. Crowell, 1967. Grades 5 and up.

    When a full-blooded Cherokee, Watie, obtains rifles for the Confederates, Jefferson Davis Busey, a Union soldier, must spy on the Rebels.

Levy, Mimi Cooper. *Corrie and the Yankee*. Illustrated by Ernest Crichlow. New York: Viking Press, 1959. Grades 4 and up.

    Corrie is a young black girl on a Southern plantation. She becomes involved in the war when she rescues a wounded Yankee soldier.

Lunn, Janet. *The Root Cellar*. New York: Charles Scribner's Sons, 1981. Grades 5 and up.

    Rose is unhappily spending the summer with Canadian relatives. Taking refuge in a root cellar, she finds herself thrust into the 1860s and the Civil War.

Monjo, F. N. *Gettysburg: Tad Lincoln's Story*. Illustrated by Douglas Gorsline. New York: E. P. Dutton, Inc., 1976. Grades 3 and up.

    This is the fictionalized account of the three-day battle of Gettysburg as Tad Lincoln might have told it.

———. *The Vicksburg Veteran*. Illustrated by Douglas Gorsline. New York: Simon and Schuster, 1971. Grades 2 and up.

    Twelve-year-old Fred Grant is with his father, Ulysses S. Grant, during the Battle of Vicksburg. With simple text and black-and-white illustrations, the reader learns how Fred becomes a Vicksburg veteran.

Moore, S. E. *Secret Island*. Illustrated by Judith Gwyn Brown. New York: Four Winds Press, 1977. Grades 4 and up.

    To cheer up young John, Captain Gray gives him an assignment as a special agent looking for escaped Rebel prisoners. Surprisingly, John becomes involved with secret codes, spies, and mystery.

O'Dell, Scott. *The 290*. Boston: Houghton Mifflin Company, 1976. Grades 4 and up.

    Jim Lynne signed on with the crew of the *290*, which unexpectedly became the *Alabama*, an important Confederate war vessel.

Reeder, Carolyn. *Shades of Gray*. New York: Macmillan Publishing Company, 1989. Grades 4 and up.

    Will Page has lost his entire family to the Civil War, and now he must live with his Uncle Jed, who refused to fight the hated Yankees. Will must come to grips with his growing respect for Uncle Jed while resenting his noninvolvement in the war.

Reit, Seymour. *Behind Civil Lines: The Incredible Story of Emma Edmonds, Civil War Spy*. San Diego: Harcourt Brace Jovanovich, 1988. Grades 3 and up.

    Emma Edmonds disguises herself as a man, joins the Union Army, and infiltrates the Confederate Army.

Steele, William O. *The Perilous Road*. New York: Harcourt Brace and World, 1958. Grades 4 and up.

Though Chris's brother joined the Northern army and his parents maintain neutrality, Chris continues to hate the Yankees. His report of a Yankee supply train endangers his brother, bringing home the futility of the war.

Wormser, Richard. *The Black Mustanger*. Illustrated by Don Bolognese. New York: William Morrow and Company, 1971. Grades 4 and up.

This story of a boy and his half-black, half-Apache mentor is set in the post-Civil War period in Texas.

6
The Northeast

Northeast states:
- Connecticut
- Maine
- Massachusetts
- New Hampshire
- Rhode Island
- Vermont

Chapter Six
Word List

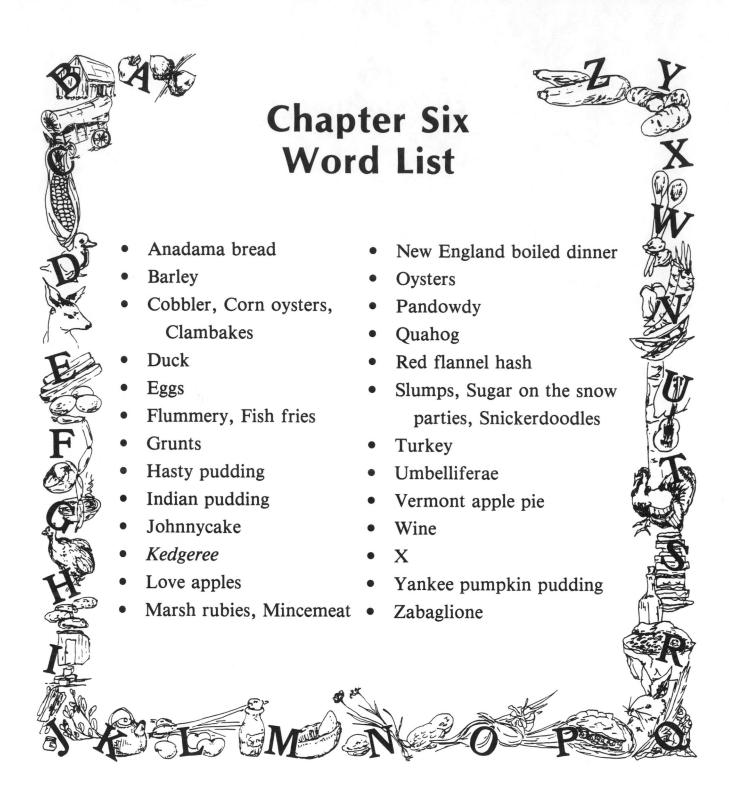

- Anadama bread
- Barley
- Cobbler, Corn oysters, Clambakes
- Duck
- Eggs
- Flummery, Fish fries
- Grunts
- Hasty pudding
- Indian pudding
- Johnnycake
- *Kedgeree*
- Love apples
- Marsh rubies, Mincemeat

- New England boiled dinner
- Oysters
- Pandowdy
- Quahog
- Red flannel hash
- Slumps, Sugar on the snow parties, Snickerdoodles
- Turkey
- Umbelliferae
- Vermont apple pie
- Wine
- X
- Yankee pumpkin pudding
- Zabaglione

BLUEBERRY MUFFINS

Ingredients
2 cups flour
½ cup sugar
2 tablespoons baking powder
1 teaspoon baking soda
½ teaspoon salt
2 eggs
1 cup sour milk* or buttermilk
¼ cup butter, melted
1 tablespoon flour
1 cup blueberries

Steps
1. Preheat oven to 400 degrees.
2. Grease 12 muffin cups or use cupcake papers.
3. Mix together flour, sugar, baking powder, baking soda, and salt in a large mixing bowl.
4. In a small bowl mix together eggs, sour milk, and melted butter.
5. Stir liquid ingredients into dry ingredients. Mix only until dry ingredients are moistened. Do not overmix.
6. In a small bowl stir 1 tablespoon flour into blueberries.
7. Gently fold blueberries into dough.
8. Pour batter into muffin tins.
9. Bake 20 minutes or until light brown on top.
10. Serve hot with butter.

*To make sour milk, stir 1 tablespoon vinegar or lemon juice into 1 cup of milk and let stand 10 minutes to curdle.

Makes 12.

Library Link 1: Find out what a bilberry is.

FRIED DOUGH

Ingredients
1½ cups flour
1¼ teaspoons baking powder
¾ teaspoon salt
2 tablespoons shortening or lard, softened
½ cup warm water
Oil for frying
Tomato sauce, cinnamon sugar, or confectioner's sugar

Steps
1. Mix flour, baking powder, and salt.
2. Cut in shortening until mixture begins to form small balls.
3. Stir in warm water.
4. Turn dough onto a floured board and knead for 2 to 3 minutes.
5. Cover dough with a towel and let it rest for about 15 minutes.
6. Heat about ¼ inch of oil in a large frying pan to 375 degrees.
7. Divide dough into 5 equal pieces.
8. Roll each piece into a ball. Then flatten into a 5-inch circle.
9. Using a sharp knife, cut 4 1-inch slits into dough.
10. Place circles of dough carefully into hot oil.
11. Cook until brown and then turn and brown on other side.
12. Drain on paper towels.
13. Serve immediately with tomato sauce, cinnamon sugar, or confectioner's sugar.

Makes 5.

Library Link 2:   When did good-quality wheat flour become readily available?

RAISED DOUGHNUTS

Ingredients
1 package dry yeast
1 tablespoon sugar
2 tablespoons very warm water (110 to 115 degrees)
½ cup sugar
1 egg, beaten
1 cup milk
3 tablespoons melted butter
3½ to 4 cups flour
Oil for frying
Butter for greasing

Steps
1. Combine yeast, 1 tablespoon sugar, and warm water in small bowl. Stir until all yeast is dissolved.
2. Let yeast mixture stand 10 to 15 minutes or until foamy.
3. Mix ½ cup sugar, egg, milk, and melted butter in a large bowl.
4. Add yeast mixture to egg mixture and mix well.
5. Stir in 3½ cups flour to form a soft dough.
6. Add more flour if dough is too sticky.
7. Grease a large bowl and put dough in it.
8. Brush top with butter.
9. Cover bowl with plastic wrap and let rise in warm place until doubled in size.
10. Divide dough in half.
11. Roll ½ of dough out on floured board to about ½ inch thick.
12. Cut out doughnuts with a 2- to 3-inch doughnut cutter.
13. Place cut doughnuts on floured board and cover with a towel.
14. Repeat with the other half of dough.
15. Let dough rise again until doubled in size.
16. In a deep fryer heat at least 3 inches of oil until it reaches 375 degrees. Keep oil at this temperature.
17. Place doughnuts in oil and fry until browned on both sides.
18. Remove from oil and drain on paper towels.
19. Eat while warm. After they cool, they are very dry. Try dunking them in milk, coffee, or maple syrup.

Makes 12 to 15.

Library Link 3: Today we often fry in melted shortening or vegetable oil. What did the early settlers use for frying?

STEAMED CLAMS

Ingredients
5 dozen clams (littleneck or cherrystone)
Water
½ teaspoon salt
¼ pound butter

Steps
1. Rinse clams in cold water twice to remove sand and grit.
2. Pour about ½ inch of water into a large kettle.
3. Add salt and clams. Cover kettle.
4. Bring water to a boil and simmer about 10 minutes until clams open.
5. Remove clams from liquid and throw away any that did not open. Liquid may be saved and used as clam broth in other recipes.
6. Melt butter.
7. Remove clams from shells with a fork, dip in melted butter, and eat.

Serves 5.

Library Link 4: A clam is a bivalved mollusk. What does bivalved mean?

FRIED CLAMS

Ingredients
¾ cup milk
¾ cup evaporated milk
1 large egg
¾ teaspoon vanilla
¼ teaspoon salt
Dash of pepper
4½ dozen clams, removed from shell (littleneck, cherrystone, or Ipswich)
⅔ cup flour
1⅔ cup cornmeal
Oil for frying

Steps
1. Combine milk, evaporated milk, egg, vanilla, salt, and pepper.
2. Clams may be kept whole or cut into smaller pieces.
3. Soak clams in milk mixture.
4. Combine flour and cornmeal in a small bowl.
5. Drop clams into flour and cornmeal mixture and turn until coated.
6. Heat oil to 375 degrees.
7. Fry clams in oil until browned on both sides.
8. Drain on paper towels.
9. Serve immediately.

Serves 5.

Library Link 5: Which type of clam is larger, littleneck or cherrystone?

CORN OYSTERS

Ingredients
1 large egg
1 cup whole-kernel corn
½ teaspoon salt
¼ teaspoon pepper
⅓ cup flour
2 tablespoons milk
Oil for frying

Steps
1. Beat egg in medium-size bowl.
2. Drain corn and add to egg.
3. Stir in salt, pepper, flour, and milk until mixture is well combined.
4. Pour oil about ¼ inch deep in a large frying pan.
5. Heat oil over medium heat.
6. Drop corn mixture by tablespoons into hot oil.
7. Fry until brown on bottom. Turn over and brown other side.
8. Serve as a vegetable or main dish with maple syrup.

Makes 10 to 12.

Library Link 6: Corn oysters were given their name because they are shaped like oysters. A similar name is given to a very different food, the coon oyster. Find out what coon oysters are and how they got their name.

RED FLANNEL HASH

Ingredients
3 medium potatoes
3 tablespoons butter
1 12-ounce can corned beef, chopped
1 1-pound can sliced beets, chopped
¼ cup chopped onion
½ cup cream
Salt and pepper, to taste

Steps
1. Boil potatoes until soft and then chop into small cubes.
2. Melt butter in a large frying pan over medium heat.
3. Put corned beef, beets, potatoes, and onion in frying pan and saute until browned.
4. Pour cream over mixture.
5. Cook for about 15 minutes or until a brown crust forms around the edges of the pan.
6. Add salt and pepper to taste.

Serves 4 to 5.

Library Link 7: What are the other meanings for the word *hash*?

NEW ENGLAND CLAM CHOWDER

Ingredients
8-ounce can or jar chopped clams in clam juice
4 strips raw bacon
1 small onion
2 large potatoes
½ teaspoon salt
¼ teaspoon pepper
1½ cups milk
⅓ cup light cream
1½ tablespoons milk
1 tablespoon flour

Steps
1. Drain clams and save juice.
2. Cook the bacon in a large saucepan over medium-high heat until crisp.
3. Drain bacon on paper towel.
4. Chop onion.
5. Add onion to bacon grease and cook until clear.
6. Peel potatoes and chop into small cubes.
7. Add potatoes to onion.
8. Pour clam juice into a measuring cup and add water until it equals 1 cup.
9. Add clam juice to saucepan with potatoes and onions and cook over medium heat until potatoes are tender.
10. Add salt, pepper, 1½ cups milk, and light cream to saucepan.
11. Add the 1½ tablespoons of milk to the 1 tablespoon of flour in a small bowl and stir until well mixed.
12. Slowly stir the flour mixture into the saucepan and turn heat to medium high. Keep stirring until the mixture just starts to boil.
13. Remove from heat immediately.
14. Taste and add more salt and pepper if desired.
15. When reheating chowder, do not boil.

Serves 6.

Library Link 8: List as many types of clams as you can.

HARVARD BEETS

Ingredients
8 large beets
⅔ cup sugar
2 teaspoons cornstarch
⅓ cup water
¼ cup vinegar
4 tablespoons butter
Salt and pepper, to taste

Steps
1. Peel beets and cook in boiling water until tender.
2. Cool beets and cut into slices about ¼ inch thick.
3. Mix sugar and cornstarch.
4. Add sugar and cornstarch to water and mix well.
5. Pour mixture into a saucepan and add vinegar.
6. Boil over medium-high heat for 5 minutes.
7. Add beets, stir, and let stand 30 minutes to 1 hour with heat off.
8. To serve, bring to a boil and stir in butter, salt, and pepper.

Serves 6.

Library Link 9: What part of the beet plant is eaten?

CRANBERRY SAUCE

Ingredients
1 pound cranberries
2½ cups sugar
½ cup molasses or maple syrup

Steps
1. Wash cranberries and remove stems.
2. Put cranberries in saucepan and add about ½ inch of water.
3. Bring to a boil and simmer over low heat about 15 minutes, until cranberries are soft.
4. Stir sugar and molasses into cranberries and remove from heat.
5. May be served either hot or cold.

Serves 8.

Library Link 10: How did cranberries get their name?

APPLE PANDOWDY

Ingredients
Pastry

1 cup flour

½ teaspoon salt

¼ cup shortening

¼ cup cold water

Filling

8 large apples

½ cup sugar

½ teaspoon cinnamon

¼ teaspoon nutmeg

1/8 teaspoon cloves

1/8 teaspoon salt

⅓ cup molasses

Water

3 tablespoons melted butter

3 tablespoons molasses

Cream

Steps
Pastry

1. Mix flour and salt.
2. Cut in shortening with a pastry blender.
3. Add water and stir lightly until dough pulls away from sides of bowl.
4. Put dough onto a floured board.
5. Pat out into a small square.
6. Cut off ⅔ of the dough and roll into a strip about 3 inches wide and 25 inches long.
7. Arrange strip to fit around the inside wall of a 1½-quart casserole dish. Do not cover the bottom of the dish. Make sure pastry is about ½ inch higher than the edge of the casserole dish.
8. Preheat oven to 425 degrees.

Filling

1. Peel, core, and cut apples into quarters.
2. In a large bowl combine apples, sugar, cinnamon, nutmeg, cloves, and salt.
3. Put the ⅓ cup molasses in a measuring cup and add enough water to make ½ cup.
4. Add molasses mixture to apple mixture.
5. Stir in melted butter.
6. Pour apple mixture into casserole dish.
7. Roll out the rest of the pastry so that it is a little bit larger than the top of the casserole dish.
8. Place pastry on top of apple mixture and press top pastry to side pastry, tucking in edges around the inside of the dish.
9. Bake at 425 degrees for 20 to 25 minutes or until crust is light brown.
10. Remove from oven.
11. Turn oven down to 350 degrees.
12. Take 2 knives and cut crust up into pieces by crisscrossing the crust.
13. Cover casserole dish and put it back in the oven for 20 more minutes.
14. Remove dish from oven, uncover, and drizzle 3 tablespoons molasses over the top.
15. Bake uncovered for 10 more minutes.
16. Serve warm with or without cream.

Serves 8.

Library Link 11:   Find the meaning of the word *pandowdy*.

PUMPKIN PIE

Ingredients
1 9-inch pie shell
1 small cooking pumpkin
3 eggs
1¾ cups evaporated milk
½ cup molasses
¼ cup sugar
¼ teaspoon salt
2 tablespoons cinnamon
1 tablespoon ginger
½ teaspoon cloves
½ teaspoon allspice

Steps
1. Cut pumpkin into about 8 small chunks.
2. Peel off outside skin.
3. Remove seeds.
4. Simmer in a saucepan with water until pumpkin is tender. Drain.
5. Force pumpkin through a food mill.
6. Use 2 to 2½ cups of strained pumpkin for pie. The rest may be frozen for another use.
7. Beat eggs in a large bowl.
8. Add pumpkin, milk, molasses, sugar, salt, cinnamon, ginger, cloves, and allspice. Stir well.
9. Pour pumpkin mixture into pie shell.
10. Bake at 400 degrees for 15 minutes.
11. Turn oven down to 375 degrees and cook for 30 more minutes or until a knife inserted in the center comes out clean.

Serves 8.

Library Link 12:   Why did the American Indians plant pumpkin with corn?

BIBLIOGRAPHY—THE NORTHEAST

Nonfiction

Bernheim, Marc, and Evelyn Bernheim. *Growing Up in Old New England*. New York: Macmillan Publishing Company, 1971. Grades 3 and up.
   Black-and-white photographs of children in Old Sturbridge Village demonstrate life in the 1820s.

Gemming, Elizabeth. *Blow Ye Winds Westerly: The Seaports and Sailing of Old New England*. New York: Thomas Y. Crowell, 1971. Grades 4 and up.
   The role of the sea in the development of New England is explored in Gemming's description of Old Salem, Boston Town, Cape Cod, Nantucket, and New Bedford. A glossary, complete index, and photographs enhance the text.

_____. *The Cranberry Book*. New York: Coward-McCann, Inc., 1983. Grades 4 and up.

Gemming describes the contribution of the cranberry to the diet of the colonists, as well as its cultivation and harvesting.

Gibbons, Gail. *From Path to Highway: The Story of the Boston Post Road*. New York: Thomas Y. Crowell, 1986. Grades 1 and up.

Watercolor illustrations and simple text tell the history of the road from its days as an Indian trail to the present.

Graymont, Barbara. *Indians of North America: The Iroquois*. New York: Chelsea House Publishers, 1988. Grades 4 and up.

In upstate New York, the Iroquois lived and fought alongside many other tribes. Their history and struggle for survival are described with black-and-white and color photographs.

Jennings, Jerry E., editor. *Northeast*. Grand Rapids, Mich.: The Fieldler Company, 1977. Grades 4 and up.

Extensive discussions of many aspects of the Northeast are included, along with numerous pictures, charts, and maps.

Phelan, Mary Kay. *Waterway West: The Story of the Erie Canal*. Illustrated by David Frampton. New York: Thomas Y. Crowell, 1977. Grades 4 and up.

The Erie Canal, America's first major waterway, opened in 1825, linking the Hudson River and the Great Lakes. Using journals and letters, Phelan describes the development of the canal.

Tunis, Edwin. *The Young United States: 1783-1830*. New York: Thomas Y. Crowell, 1969. Grades 4 and up.

Tunis writes about and illustrates the changes that occurred after the end of the Revolutionary War. He describes the people, regional life, government, commerce, schools, travel, the arts, and the country's expansion.

Weinstein-Farson, Laurie. *Indians of North America: The Wampanoag*. New York: Chelsea House Publishers, 1989. Grades 4 and up.

The two-hundred-year struggle and survival of this tribe, which lived along the shores of Cape Cod, is described with text and a variety of photographs.

Fiction

Alcott, Louisa May. *An Old Fashioned Thanksgiving*. Illustrated by Holly Johnson. Philadelphia: J. B. Lippincott, 1974. Grades 2 and up.

The Bassets are preparing for Thanksgiving when word comes that their grandmother is ill. The parents leave, and the children continue to prepare for the feast.

Cooney, Barbara. *Island Boy*. New York: Viking Penguin Inc., 1988. All ages.

Matthais's family built their home on Tibbetts Island, and Matthais learned about all that the island had to offer, returning to it throughout his life.

Fritz, Jean. *I, Adam*. Illustrated by Peter Burchard. New York: Coward McCann and Geoghegan, 1963. Grades 5 and up.

Adam lives in New England in the mid-1800s and must decide his life goals.

Jacob, Helen Pierce. *The Diary of the Strawbridge Place*. New York: Atheneum, 1978. Grades 3 and up.
    Thirteen-year-old twins live on a farm that is the last stop on the Underground Railway. When a search party arrives, the twins delay it so the slaves can continue their journey.

Lord, Athena. *A Spirit to Ride the Whirlwind*. New York: Macmillan Publishing Company, 1981. Grades 5 and up.
    In Lowell, Massachusetts, female mill workers take great risks to organize a union.

McCurdy, Michael. *Hannah's Farm: The Seasons on an Early American Homestead*. New York: Holiday House, 1988. All ages.
    The seasons on a typical nineteenth-century New England homestead, Morgan Farm, are explored through Hannah's life. McCurdy's wood engravings suit the content of this book.

Peck, Robert Newton. *A Day No Pigs Would Die*. New York: Alfred A. Knopf, Inc., 1972. Grades 6 and up.
    A boy in Vermont faces the realities of farm life in this poignant story.

Roop, Peter, and Connie Roop. *Keep the Lights Burning, Abbie*. Illustrated by Peter E. Hanson. Minneapolis, Minn.: Carolrhoda Books, 1985. Grades 1 and up.
    When a storm hits the Maine coast in 1856, Abbie must keep the lighthouse lamps burning.

Speare, Elizabeth George. *The Sign of the Beaver*. Boston: Houghton Mifflin Company, 1983. Grades 3 and up.
    A young boy survives two seasons in the Northeast woods while his father returns to their former home for his wife and younger children. Unexpected help from Indians leads to a dilemma when the Indians are forced out of their lands.

_____. *The Witch of Blackbird Pond*. New York: Dell Publishing Company, Inc., 1972. Grades 5 and up.
    When Kit moves from the Caribbean to the New England coast, she is unprepared for the drab existence, treatment of suspected witches, and general loneliness.

Stevenson, Drew. *The Ballad of Penelope Lou ... and Me*. Trumansburg, N.Y.: Crossing Press, 1978. Grades 1 and up.
    After sailing all over the world in the late 1800s, Penelope Lou returns to the coast of New England. She is determined to marry a brave man who loves the water, but when she marries one who fears the water she respects his preferences.

Turkle, Brinton. *Rachel and Obadiah*. New York: E. P. Dutton, Inc., 1978. Grades K and up.
    Rachel wants to be the runner who lets the neighborhood know when a ship is arriving at Nantucket Island and must race against her brother to earn the privilege.

Wriston, Hildreth. *Susan's Secret*. Illustrated by W. T. Mars. New York: Farrar, Straus and Giroux, Inc., 1957. Grades 4 and up.
    Susan lives in Vermont. When her family leaves, she guides slaves on the Underground Railroad.

7
The Mid-Atlantic States

Mid-Atlantic States:

Delaware

Maryland

New Jersey

New York

Pennsylvania

Chapter Seven
Word List

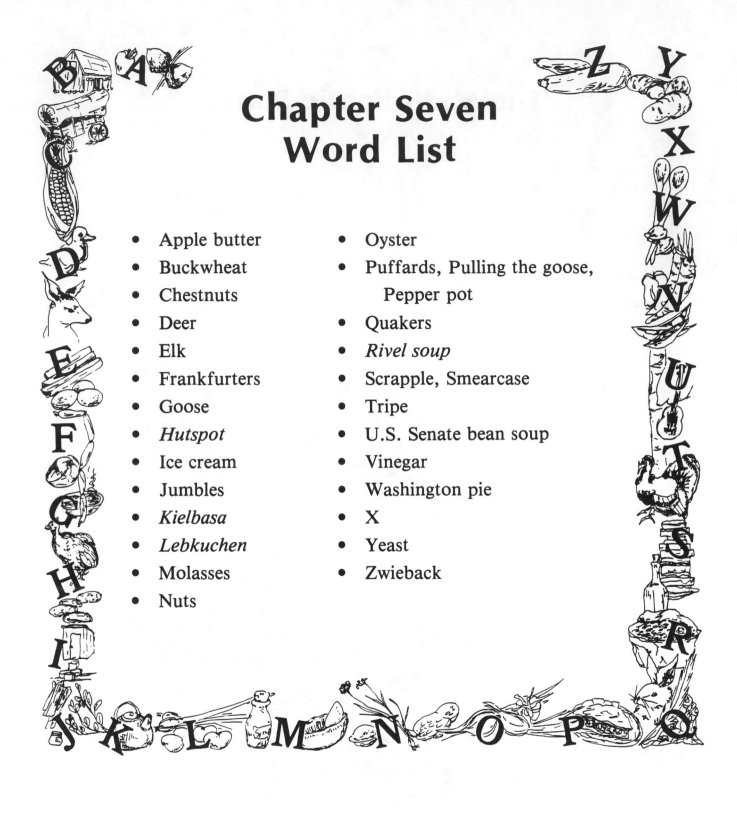

- Apple butter
- Buckwheat
- Chestnuts
- Deer
- Elk
- Frankfurters
- Goose
- *Hutspot*
- Ice cream
- Jumbles
- *Kielbasa*
- *Lebkuchen*
- Molasses
- Nuts
- Oyster
- Puffards, Pulling the goose, Pepper pot
- Quakers
- *Rivel soup*
- Scrapple, Smearcase
- Tripe
- U.S. Senate bean soup
- Vinegar
- Washington pie
- X
- Yeast
- Zwieback

JEWISH RYE BREAD

Ingredients

Starter

1 package dry yeast
½ teaspoon sugar

2 cups very warm water (110 to 115 degrees)
2¼ cups rye flour

Sponge

1 package dry yeast
¾ cup very warm water
1 cup white flour

Pinch of sugar
1 cup rye flour

Dough

1 tablespoon salt
2½ cups white flour
1 egg white

4 tablespoons caraway seeds
Yellow cornmeal
1 teaspoon water

Steps

Starter

1. Dissolve 1 package of yeast in 2 cups very warm water.
2. Stir in sugar and rye flour.
3. Cover and let stand at room temperature for 24 hours. Mixture will smell sour.

Sponge

1. Dissolve 1 package of yeast and the pinch of sugar in ¼ cup of the warm water.
2. Let stand until foamy.
3. In a large mixing bowl, combine starter and all ingredients for sponge. Stir well.
4. Cover and let stand for 4 hours. Stir mixture.

Dough

1. Add salt, caraway seeds, and remaining white flour. Stir well.
2. Put dough onto a floured board. Knead for 10 minutes. Add extra flour if dough gets sticky.
3. Grease a large bowl. Roll dough around in it to grease dough.
4. Cover and let rise until dough has doubled in size (1 to 2 hours).
5. Sprinkle cornmeal on a large cookie sheet.
6. Form dough into 2 long loaves and put them on the cornmeal.
7. Let loaves rise until they double in size (1 to 2 hours).
8. Preheat oven to 425 degrees.
9. Place a pan containing 1 to 2 inches of hot water on the bottom rack of the oven.
10. Mix egg white with 1 teaspoon water. Beat well.
11. Brush egg white mixture on top of loaves.
12. Bake loaves 20 minutes.
13. Turn oven down to 375 degrees and bake 15 minutes more or until the loaves make a hollow sound when tapped.
14. Cool loaves before slicing.
15. Wrap tightly after loaves have cooled.

Makes 2 loaves.

Library Link 1: Rye is grown in Pennsylvania. What other grains are grown in Pennsylvania?

SOFT PRETZELS

Ingredients
1 package dry yeast
1½ teaspoons sugar
1 cup very warm water (110 to 115 degrees)
2½ cups flour
1 teaspoon salt
2 tablespoons baking soda
1 to 2 tablespoons coarse salt
Cornmeal
Mustard (optional)

Steps
1. In a small bowl, dissolve yeast and sugar in ¼ cup of the very warm water.
2. In a large bowl, mix the flour and salt. Then stir in the remaining ¾ cup of the water.
3. When yeast mixture is foamy, add it to the flour mixture and mix thoroughly.
4. Put the mixture on a floured board and let it rest for 5 minutes.
5. Wash and dry the large bowl. Grease it well.
6. Knead dough 10 to 15 minutes, adding more flour if sticky.
7. Put dough in greased bowl and cover tightly with plastic wrap.
8. Let dough rise 1 hour or until doubled in size.
9. Punch dough down.
10. Cut dough into 8 pieces.
11. Roll each piece into a thin rope 20 to 24 inches long.
12. To shape the pretzel, grab each end of the rope and form a horseshoe shape with the curved part away from you.
13. Twist the ends around each other and press firmly onto the loop of dough beneath them.
14. Let pretzels rest on a floured board, under a towel, for 15 minutes.
15. Preheat oven to 450 degrees.
16. Simmer a quart of water in a medium pan. Add baking soda.
17. Carefully place a few pretzels at a time in water for 30 seconds on each side.
18. Remove pretzels from water. Pat dry with a towel.
19. Lightly dust a baking sheet with cornmeal.
20. Place pretzels on baking sheet and sprinkle with coarse salt.
21. Bake 10 to 12 minutes or until light brown.
22. Serve warm with mustard on top.

Makes 8.

Library Link 2:   When were the first commercial pretzel bakeries established?

MATZOH BALL SOUP

Ingredients
1 quart chicken stock
4 eggs
¼ cup oil
½ teaspoon baking powder
1½ cups matzoh meal
1 teaspoon chopped parsley
¼ teaspoon salt

Steps
1. Pour chicken stock into a large saucepan and boil.
2. Beat eggs in a large mixing bowl.
3. Add oil to eggs. Beat well.
4. Slowly stir in baking powder, matzoh meal, parsley, and salt.
5. Wet hands and shape mixture into small balls.
6. Drop balls into simmering chicken stock.
7. Cook about 20 minutes, until balls are firm and cooked through.

Serves 5 to 6.

Library Link 3: When are matzoh balls often eaten by Jewish people?

MARYLAND FRIED OYSTERS

Ingredients
2 dozen shucked oysters
2 eggs
2 tablespoons milk
1 teaspoon salt
¼ teaspoon pepper
1 cup dried bread crumbs
Margarine for frying
Tartar sauce

Steps
1. Wash oysters and pat dry.
2. Beat eggs in a small bowl.
3. Add milk, salt, and pepper. Mix well.
4. Dip oysters in egg mixture. Dip in bread crumbs.
5. Melt margarine in a large frying pan over medium heat.
6. Cook breaded oysters in margarine until browned on both sides.
7. Serve with tartar sauce.

Serves 4.

Library Link 4: Study a map of Maryland. Why were oysters so plentiful in that area?

MARYLAND CRAB CAKES

Ingredients

3 tablespoons butter or margarine
3 tablespoons chopped onions
1⅔ cups soft bread crumbs
1½ pounds crab meat
2 eggs

½ teaspoon dry mustard
Salt, pepper, and paprika to taste
½ cup flour
Butter for frying

Steps

1. Melt 3 tablespoons butter in a large saucepan over medium heat.
2. Cook onion in butter until soft and clear.
3. Remove from heat.
4. Stir in bread crumbs, crab meat, eggs, mustard, salt, pepper, and paprika.
5. If the mixture is too dry, add a little milk.
6. Shape mixture into flat cakes.
7. Roll cakes in flour.
8. Melt butter in a frying pan over medium heat.
9. Fry both sides of crab cake until well browned and cooked through.

Serves 6.

Library Link 5: What are soft-shell crabs?

SOUTH PHILLY CHEESE STEAK SANDWICHES

Ingredients

4 tablespoons margarine
2 large onions
12 frozen sandwich steaks (the thin, leathery sandwich steaks)
6 Italian rolls, sliced lengthwise
6 slices American cheese
Salt or ketchup

Steps

1. Heat a large griddle over medium heat.
2. Melt margarine on griddle.
3. Slice onions and cook on griddle.
4. As the onion slices turn soft and brown, push them over to the edges of the griddle.
5. Put the sandwich steaks on the griddle and cook until browned on both sides.
6. Put 1 slice of cheese on every other piece of steak. Melt cheese.
7. Put one cheese-covered steak on top of another steak. Add onions. Place in a roll.
8. Add salt and ketchup, if desired.

Makes 6.

Library Link 6: For many years, Jersey and Guernsey cows gave the milk and the cream used for cheese production. What kind of cows are used now? Why?

SNICKERDOODLES

Ingredients

½ cup butter, softened
¾ cup sugar
1 egg
2 cups flour
1¼ teaspoons baking powder
½ teaspoon salt
½ cup milk
1 teaspoon vanilla
¼ cup sugar
1 tablespoon cinnamon

Steps

1. Preheat oven to 325 degrees.
2. Stir butter with a wooden spoon until creamy.
3. Add sugar. Mix well.
4. Add egg. Mix well.
5. Mix flour, baking powder, and salt in a separate bowl.
6. Add one third of the flour mixture to butter mixture. Stir well.
7. Add half of the milk to the butter mixture. Stir well.
8. Add half of the remaining flour mixture and half of the milk. Stir well.
9. Stir in the vanilla.
10. Add the remaining flour mixture. Stir well.
11. Drop heaping teaspoonfuls of dough about 2 inches apart onto a greased cookie sheet.
12. Mix ¼ cup sugar and 1 tablespoon cinnamon in a small bowl.
13. Sprinkle sugar and cinnamon mixture over the mounds of dough.
14. Bake 10 to 15 minutes or until cookies are lightly browned around the edges.
15. Cool. Store in a tightly covered container.

Makes 3 to 4 dozen cookies.

Library Link 7: These are Dutch drop cookies. Where did the name *Snickerdoodles* come from?

PENNSYLVANIA DUTCH SHOO-FLY PIE

Ingredients
1 9-inch unbaked pie shell

Molasses mixture
½ teaspoon baking soda
¾ cup hot water
¾ cup molasses

Crumb mixture
1½ cups flour
¾ cup brown sugar
½ teaspoon cinnamon
¼ teaspoon nutmeg
¼ teaspoon ginger
¼ cup butter

Steps
1. Stir baking soda into hot water until it dissolves.
2. Add molasses. Stir well.
3. Pour a third of this mixture into the pie shell.
4. Mix the flour, brown sugar, cinnamon, nutmeg, and ginger well.
5. Cut in the butter until mixture is crumbly.
6. Sprinkle one-third of the crumb mixture over the molasses mixture in the pie shell.
7. Repeat with half of the remaining molasses mixture and half the remaining crumb mixture.
8. Use the remaining portions of each mixture to make a third set of layers.
9. Bake pie at 425 degrees for 10 minutes.
10. Reduce heat to 350 degrees. Bake for 30 minutes.

Serves 8.

Library Link 8: How did this pie get its name?

NEW YORK CHEESECAKE

Ingredients

Crust
1 cup flour
⅓ cup sugar
½ teaspoon vanilla
8 tablespoons softened butter
1 egg yolk

Filling
24 ounces cream cheese, softened
1 cup sugar
4 eggs
3 tablespoons sour cream
1 teaspoon grated lemon rind
2 tablespoons flour
½ teaspoon vanilla

Steps

Crust
1. Combine flour, sugar, and vanilla in a large mixing bowl.
2. Mix in butter and egg yolk until mixture forms a soft dough. Add a small amount of cold water if dough is too dry. Do not overmix.
3. Chill dough 1 hour in refrigerator.
4. Preheat oven to 400 degrees.
5. Grease the bottom and sides of a 9-inch springform pan.
6. Roll out dough on a floured board.
7. Using the bottom of the pan as a guide, cut out a circle of dough.
8. Press the circle of dough onto the bottom of the pan.
9. Press the rest of the dough evenly onto the sides of the pan.
10. Bake the dough 15 minutes. Remove from oven.
11. Reduce the oven temperature to 275 degrees.

Filling
1. Beat cream cheese with an electric mixer until smooth.
2. Beat in sugar, eggs, sour cream, lemon rind, flour, and vanilla. Pour cream cheese mixture into cooled crust.
3. Bake at 275 degrees one hour.
4. Turn off oven and let cheesecake sit in oven for 15 more minutes.
5. Remove from oven. Cool completely before serving.

Note: To soften cream cheese, let stand at room temperature one to two hours.

Serves 8 to 10.

Library Link 9: Cheesecake came from the Germans, who often used zwieback for the crust. What is zwieback?

MINEHAHA CAKE

Ingredients

Cake
½ cup butter, softened
2 cups sugar
2½ teaspoons baking powder
¾ cup milk
1⅔ cups flour
5 egg whites at room temperature

Icing
2 cups sugar
3 tablespoons water
2 egg whites at room temperature
Dash salt
¾ cup raisins
¾ cup walnuts
1 teaspoon vanilla

Steps

Cake
1. Preheat oven to 350 degrees.
2. Cream butter with a wooden spoon.
3. Stir in sugar and baking powder.
4. Divide milk and flour into 3 equal parts. Begin with the flour and alternately beat in each part.
5. Put egg whites in a medium-sized glass or metal bowl.
6. Add a dash of salt.
7. Whip with an electric mixer on high until soft peaks form.
8. Gently fold flour mixture into the egg whites until well mixed.
9. Grease 2 9-inch round cake pans.
10. Pour cake batter into the pans.
11. Bake about 25 minutes or until done in the center.
12. Let cool.

Icing
1. Put sugar and water in a heavy, medium-sized saucepan.
2. Boil over medium-high heat until the mixture drops from a spoon, forming a hair.
3. Put egg whites in a small bowl with high sides.
4. Add salt.
5. Whip until the egg whites are thick and foamy.
6. Pour sugar over the egg whites and beat until thick.
7. Add raisins, walnuts, and vanilla. Stir well.
8. After cake cools spread icing between the layers and on the top.

Serves 10 to 12.

Library Link 10: What Dutch man explored Delaware in 1609?

PENNSYLVANIA DUTCH APPLE MERINGUE

Ingredients

3 to 4 large apples
Water
⅓ cup sugar
2 tablespoons butter
½ teaspoon nutmeg
½ teaspoon cinnamon
1 tablespoon lemon juice
3 eggs
⅓ cup powdered sugar
1 teaspoon vanilla

Steps

1. Preheat oven to 400 degrees.
2. Peel, core, and slice apples.
3. Place apples in a medium saucepan with about 1 inch of water.
4. Cook over medium heat until apples are soft.
5. Put 2 heaping cups of apples in a large mixing bowl.
6. Stir in sugar, butter, nutmeg, cinnamon, and lemon juice.
7. Separate egg yolks from egg whites.
8. Beat egg yolks.
9. Add the apple mixture. Beat well.
10. Grease a 9-inch square baking pan.
11. Pour apple mixture into greased pan.
12. Bake in oven for 15 minutes.
13. While mixture is baking, put egg whites into a medium-sized glass or metal bowl.
14. Beat egg whites with an electric mixer on high until stiff.
15. Slowly add powdered sugar and vanilla. Continue to beat until completely mixed in. This is meringue.
16. Remove apple mixture from oven after 15 minutes.
17. Pour meringue over the top of the apple mixture.
18. Reduce the oven temperature to 325 degrees.
19. Return the pan to the oven.
20. Bake until the meringue is slightly browned.
21. Cool and cut into rectangles.

Makes 12 bars.

Library Link 11: Why do many Pennsylvania Dutch have hex signs on their barns?

DELAWARE SNOW CREAM

Ingredients
1 egg
1 can evaporated milk, chilled
2 teaspoons vanilla
¾ cup sugar
Snow

Steps
1. Beat egg in a large mixing bowl.
2. Beat in the milk, vanilla, and sugar.
3. Find some fresh, clean snow.
4. Carefully fold snow into the egg mixture until the snow cream is the desired texture.

Serves 3 to 6.

Library Link 12: What U.S. president's wife made ice cream the official White House dessert?

BIBLIOGRAPHY—MID-ATLANTIC STATES

Nonfiction

Costabel, Eva Deutsch. *The Pennsylvania Dutch: Craftsmen and Farmers*. New York: Atheneum, 1986.
    Grades 3 and up.
    Costabel describes the life of a Pennsylvania Dutch farm family, thoroughly discussing their crafts and home.

Fisher, Leonard Everett. *Ellis Island: Gateway to the New World*. New York: Holiday House, 1986.
    Grades 4 and up.
    First purchased from the Indians in 1634, Ellis Island was a fort before it became an immigration station. Fisher uses actual accounts and photographs and drawings to tell the story of the immigrants who came through Ellis Island.

Graymont, Barbara. *Indians of North America: The Iroquois*. New York: Chelsea House Publishers, 1988.
    Grades 4 and up.
    In upstate New York, the Iroquois lived and fought alongside many other tribes. Their history and struggle for survival are described in black-and-white and color photographs.

Fiction

Baker, Betty. *The Night Spider Case*. New York: Farrar, Straus and Giroux, Inc., 1984. Grades 4 and up.
    New York City is the setting for this exciting adventure at the turn of the century.

Brady, Esther Wood. *The Toad on Capitol Hill*. New York: Crown Publishers, Inc., 1978. Grades 4 and up.
    Dorsy escapes a difficult stepfamily. A wish on a supposedly magic white toad makes her wonder if her wish will bring the British to Washington during the War of 1812.

Colver, Anne. *Bread-and-Butter Journey*. New York: Holt, Rinehart and Winston, 1970. Grades 2 and up.

Following *Bread-and-Butter Indian* (see Colver annotation, chapter 1), Barbara, her mother, and another family set off for western Pennsylvania with only her brother and another young boy as guides. This is based on the history of Colver's husband's family.

De Angeli, Marguerite. *Henner's Lydia*. Garden City, N.Y.: Doubleday and Company, Inc., 1963. Grades 3 and up.

De Angeli tells the story of an Amish child and her family and their life on a farm in Pennsylvania.

Flory, Jane. *The Liberation of Clementine Tipton*. Boston: Houghton Mifflin Company, 1974. Grades 2 and up.

It is 1876 in Philadelphia, and Clementine decides she prefers ponies and cleaning horses' stalls to behaving like a proper young lady.

Fritz, Jean. *The Cabin Faced West*. Illustrated by Feodor Rojankovsky. New York: Coward-McCann, Inc., 1958. Grades 3 and up.

Ann learns of the hardships and pleasures of life in a cabin in the western Pennsylvania wilderness. This is based on the life of Fritz's great-great-grandmother.

Hall, Donald. *Ox-cart Man*. Illustrated by Barbara Cooney. New York: Viking Press, 1979. All ages.

A New England farmer of the nineteenth century takes his family's produce to market, selling even his cart and ox to begin another year.

Moskin, Marietta D. *Day of the Blizzard*. Illustrated by Stephen Gammell. New York: G. P. Putnam's Sons, 1978. Grades 3 and up.

A young girl survives the blizzard of 1888 in New York City.

Rappaport, Doreen. *Trouble at the Mines*. Illustrated by Joan Sandin. New York: Thomas Y. Crowell, 1987. Grades 2 and up.

This is based on the true story of the 1898 miners' strike in Arnst, Pennsylvania. The story is about Rosie, who marched with Mother Jones, the miners' angel.

Sterling, Dorothy. *Freedom Train: The Story of Harriet Tubman*. New York: Scholastic Book Services, 1954. Grades 5 and up.

Harriet Tubman's story opens in 1827 in Maryland, when she is seven years old. Her escape to the North and her dedication to helping others use the Underground Railroad provides an exciting story.

Stevens, Carla. *Anna, Grandpa, and the Big Storm*. Illustrated by Margot Tomes. Boston: Houghton Mifflin Company, 1982. Grades 2 and up.

The New York City blizzard of 1888 is faced by a family.

Yolen, Jane. *The Gift of Sarah Barker*. New York: Viking Press, 1981. Grades 6 and up.

In a fictional town similar to a Shaker community, two teenagers fall in love, risking expulsion from their homes.

8
The Southeast

Southeast states:

Alabama	North Carolina
Arkansas	South Carolina
Florida	Tennessee
Georgia	Virginia
Kentucky	West Virginia
Louisiana	
Mississippi	

Chapter Eight
Word List

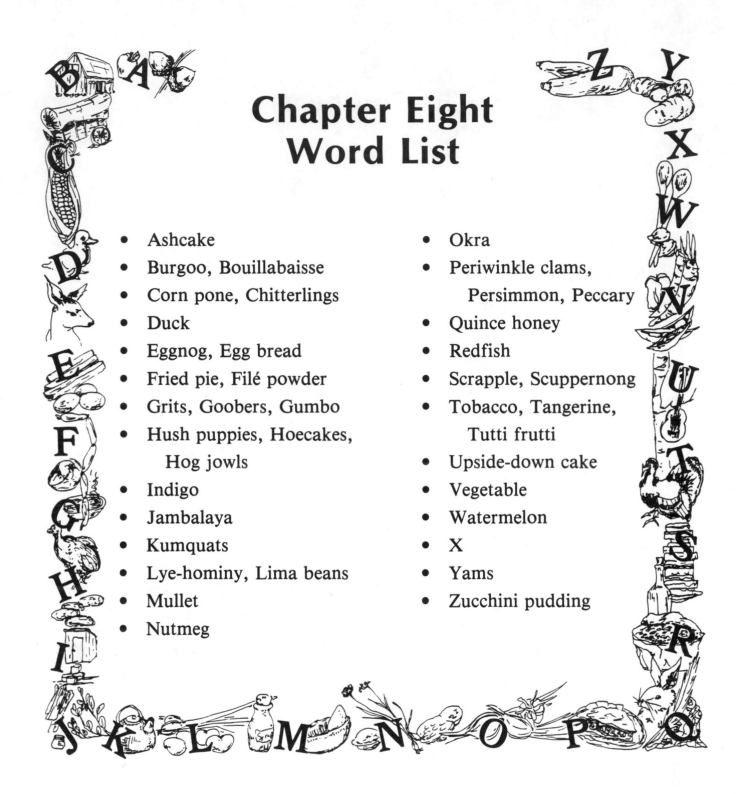

- Ashcake
- Burgoo, Bouillabaisse
- Corn pone, Chitterlings
- Duck
- Eggnog, Egg bread
- Fried pie, Filé powder
- Grits, Goobers, Gumbo
- Hush puppies, Hoecakes,
    Hog jowls
- Indigo
- Jambalaya
- Kumquats
- Lye-hominy, Lima beans
- Mullet
- Nutmeg

- Okra
- Periwinkle clams,
    Persimmon, Peccary
- Quince honey
- Redfish
- Scrapple, Scuppernong
- Tobacco, Tangerine,
    Tutti frutti
- Upside-down cake
- Vegetable
- Watermelon
- X
- Yams
- Zucchini pudding

GRITS

Ingredients
2 cups unprocessed grits
4 cups water
¾ teaspoon salt

Steps
1. Wash grits well.
2. Soak grits in water overnight.
3. Pour water off grits.
4. Put grits in a large saucepan. Add fresh water to cover.
5. Bring to a boil.
6. Add salt and cook over low heat for about 2 hours or until thickened.
7. Serve while hot.

Makes 6 cups.

Library Link 1:   What was usually served with grits for breakfast?

FRIED GRITS

Ingredients
2½ cups cooked grits
2 eggs
1 cup seasoned bread crumbs
Butter or margarine for frying

Steps
1. Pour hot, cooked grits into a loaf pan to cool.
2. Cut into slices.
3. Beat eggs in a bowl.
4. Dip slice of grits into eggs. Coat both sides.
5. Dip slice into bread crumbs. Cover both sides.
6. Heat butter in a large frying pan over medium-high heat.
7. Place slices of breaded grits into frying pan and fry on both sides until browned.
8. Add maple syrup, if desired.
9. Eat while warm.

Serves 6.

Library Link 2:   What is the source of grits?

HUSH PUPPIES

Ingredients

1¼ cups white cornmeal
1 teaspoon baking powder
1 teaspoon salt
1/8 teaspoon pepper
¾ teaspoon sugar

⅓ cup milk
¼ cup water
1 egg, beaten
Oil for frying

Steps

1. In a large bowl combine cornmeal, baking powder, salt, pepper, and sugar.
2. In a small bowl mix the milk, water, and beaten egg.
3. Pour milk mixture into cornmeal mixture and stir well.
4. Put oil in a frying pan ¼ inch deep.
5. Heat oil to 375 degrees.
6. Drop tablespoonfuls of dough into the hot oil.
7. Fry until browned on all sides.
8. Drain hush puppies on paper towels.
9. Serve warm.

Makes 16 to 20.

Library Link 3:   What is a popular theory for how hush puppies got their name?

SHORT'NIN' BREAD

Ingredients

1¼ cups butter, softened
½ cup brown sugar
¼ cup confectioner's sugar

½ teaspoon salt
½ teaspoon cinnamon
2½ cups flour

Steps

1. Cream butter.
2. Stir in both sugars and beat until creamy.
3. Add salt and cinnamon and stir well.
4. Add flour and mix well with back of a wooden spoon. If mixture becomes too stiff to stir, work it with your hands.
5. Place dough on an ungreased cookie sheet.
6. Press into a rectangle about ½ inch thick.
7. Prick dough all over with a fork.
8. Cut shallow lines into dough to mark squares.
9. Bake at 350 degrees about 15 to 20 minutes until slightly brown at the edges.
10. While still warm, cut into squares on lines you cut into the dough.
11. Remove from pan.

Makes 3 to 4 dozen.

Library Link 4:   How did butter, fat, or lard come to be called shortening?

SEAFOOD GUMBO

Ingredients

1¼ cups oil
1¼ cups flour
1½ cups chopped onion
½ cup chopped celery
¼ cup chopped green pepper
2 cloves of garlic, chopped
2 tomatoes, peeled and chopped
3 quarts chicken broth
¼ cup chopped parsley
½ teaspoon pepper
1 teaspoon salt
3 bay leaves
2 pounds small shrimp, shelled
½ pound crabmeat
2 dozen oysters and their juice
3 cups cooked rice

Steps

1. Heat 1 cup of the oil in saucepan over medium heat.
2. Add flour and stir.
3. Stir and cook over low heat for about 30 minutes until mixture, called roux, is dark brown.
4. Pour ¼ cup oil into a large soup pot.
5. Heat over medium heat. Add onion and cook until clear.
6. Add celery, green pepper, and garlic to onion. Cook 5 minutes.
7. Add roux to onion mixture and cook 10 more minutes, stirring constantly.
8. Add tomatoes to mixture.
9. Add chicken broth and turn heat to medium high.
10. Stir well and add parsley, pepper, salt, and bay leaves.
11. Bring to a boil.
12. Lower heat and simmer for 45 minutes.
13. Add shrimp and crabmeat and bring to a boil.
14. Remove from heat.
15. Chop oysters into large pieces.
16. Add oysters and their juice to mixture and stir well.
17. Remove bay leaves.
18. Put some rice in the bottom of each serving bowl and pour gumbo over it.

Serves 10.

Library Link 5: What state is most famous for its gumbo?

MASSIE STACK CAKE

Ingredients
¾ cup shortening, softened
¾ cup sugar
⅓ cup brown sugar
1 cup molasses
3 eggs
4 cups flour
½ teaspoon baking soda
¾ teaspoon salt
1 teaspoon ginger
1 cup milk
3 cups applesauce
½ teaspoon cinnamon

Steps
1. Cream shortening in a large mixing bowl.
2. Stir in sugars and molasses. Beat well.
3. Add eggs. Beat well.
4. Mix flour, baking soda, salt, and ginger in a medium bowl.
5. Add about one-third of this mixture to shortening mixture and stir well.
6. Add half the milk and stir.
7. Add half of the remaining flour mixture and stir.
8. Add the remaining milk and stir.
9. Add remaining flour mixture and stir well.
10. Grease 6 9-inch round cake pans.
11. Pour equal amounts of the batter into the 6 cake pans.
12. Bake at 375 degrees for 15 to 20 minutes or until a toothpick inserted in center comes out clean.
13. Remove cake from pans.
14. Let layers cool.
15. Stack cooled layers, putting equal amounts (about ½ cup) of applesauce between each layer.
16. Sprinkle cinnamon on top layer of applesauce and cake.

Serves 10 to 12.

Library Link 6: What special event were stack cakes used for in the South?

CHICKEN, GRAVY, AND DUMPLINGS

Ingredients

3½ to 4 pound chicken
¼ cup flour
¼ teaspoon salt
¼ cup shortening
1 small onion, chopped
1 clove garlic, chopped
1 stick celery, chopped

Salt and pepper
2 cups water
1 bay leaf
2 chicken bouillon cubes or packages
3 tablespoons flour
2 tablespoons water

Dumplings

1½ cups flour
2 teaspoons baking powder
½ teaspoon salt
¼ teaspoon pepper
1 tablespoon dried parsley
6 tablespoons cold water
½ cup shortening, softened

Steps

Chicken

1. Cut chicken into serving-sized pieces.
2. Put ¼ cup flour and ¼ teaspoon salt in a plastic bag.
3. Add the chicken pieces and shake well, coating the chicken with the flour mixture.
4. In large, heavy skillet, heat ¼ cup shortening over medium heat.
5. Add chicken to hot oil and cook until browned on both sides.
6. Remove chicken.
7. Add onion, garlic, and celery to skillet. Cook until soft.
8. Return chicken to skillet.
9. Add water, bay leaf, and bouillon. Mix.
10. Heat until it simmers.
11. Mix 3 tablespoons flour with 2 tablespoons water.
12. Stir flour mixture into simmering chicken and broth.
13. Cover and simmer for 30 minutes or until chicken is well done.

Dumplings

1. Combine flour, baking powder, salt, pepper, and parsley.
2. Cut in shortening until mixture forms balls.
3. Stir in cold water.
4. Remove cover from chicken. Drop in dumpling dough by the tablespoon on top of chicken.
5. Cover and cook 15 to 20 minutes or until dumplings are dry and cooked through.
6. Serve chicken and dumplings together with gravy over both.

Serves 6.

Library Link 7: What kind of dumplings were called blue marbles?

SWEET POTATO PIE

Ingredients
2 to 3 large sweet potatoes
½ cup butter
1 cup sugar
2 eggs
½ cup evaporated milk
1 teaspoon vanilla
¼ teaspoon salt
½ teaspoon cinnamon
½ teaspoon nutmeg
¼ teaspoon allspice
1 9-inch unbaked pie crust

Steps
1. Bake or boil sweet potatoes until soft. Peel.
2. Mash potatoes and measure. Use only 2 to 2½ cups mashed potatoes.
3. Cream butter and sugar together. Beat until light.
4. Add eggs. Mix well.
5. Stir in potatoes, milk, vanilla, salt, cinnamon, nutmeg, and allspice.
6. Pour mixture into pie crust.
7. Bake about 40 minutes at 375 degrees or until knife inserted in center comes out clean.

Serves 8.

Library Link 8: What famous king loved sweet potato pie so much he imported sweet potatoes from Spain?

PEANUT CAKE

Ingredients
Cake
1¼ cups peanut butter
½ cup margarine, softened
2 cups brown sugar
5 eggs
2 cups flour
2 teaspoons baking powder
½ teaspoon salt
¾ cup milk
2 teaspoons vanilla

Frosting
½ cup peanut butter
¼ cup margarine, softened
4 cups confectioner's sugar
½ cup milk
2 teaspoons vanilla

Steps
Cake
1. Cream peanut butter and margarine together in a large mixing bowl.
2. Add sugar and beat well.
3. Add eggs, one at a time, beating well after each one.
4. Mix flour, baking powder, and salt together in a small bowl.
5. Add one-third of the flour mixture to butters and sugar and mix well.
6. Add about half of the milk. Mix well.
7. Add half of the remaining flour mixture. Mix well.
8. Add the remaining milk. Mix well.
9. Add the remaining flour mixture. Mix well.
10. Add vanilla. Mix well.
11. Grease a 9-by-13-inch pan.
12. Pour batter into pan.
13. Bake at 350 degrees for 45 minutes or until a toothpick inserted in the center comes out clean.
14. Cool cake in pan.
15. Make frosting and frost cake.

Frosting
1. Cream peanut butter and margarine together.
2. Stir in half of the confectioner's sugar. Mix well.
3. Add the rest of the sugar.
4. Add enough milk to make a smooth frosting.
5. Stir in vanilla.
6. Beat until smooth.

Serves 12 to 15.

Library Link 9: How many tons of peanut butter do Americans eat each year?

CONFEDERATE SOLDIER CAKES

Ingredients

6 eggs
1½ cups sugar
1¼ cups candied fruit

½ cup blanched almonds
2 cups flour

Steps
1. Separate egg yolks from egg whites.
2. Beat egg yolks with an electric mixer until they are thick and lemon colored.
3. Gradually add sugar and beat well.
4. Put ½ cup flour in a small bowl and stir in candied fruit.
5. Stir fruit into egg yolk mixture.
6. In a large bowl, combine egg whites and rest of the flour.
7. Beat until thick.
8. Stir yolk mixture in. Mix well.
9. Fold in almonds.
10. Grease a 15-by-10-by-1-inch pan.
11. Pour batter into the pan.
12. Bake at 425 degrees for 10 minutes.
13. Remove from oven and cut into bars.
14. Put bars back in oven for 5 more minutes.
15. Remove from oven and cool.

Makes 24 to 32.

Library Link 10: Find out how to make candied fruit.

PECAN PIE

Ingredients

3 eggs
½ cup sugar
¼ teaspoon salt
1 cup dark corn syrup

1 teaspoon vanilla
1½ cups pecans
1 pie shell, unbaked
Whipped cream, if desired

Steps
1. Preheat oven to 450 degrees.
2. Beat eggs in a large bowl.
3. Add sugar, salt, corn syrup, and vanilla. Stir well.
4. Pour pecans into pie shell.
5. Pour egg mixture over pecans.
6. Bake in oven for 10 minutes.
7. Reduce heat to 350 degrees.
8. Bake for 35 minutes longer.
9. Remove from oven.
10. Add whipped cream if desired. Eat warm or cold.

Serves 8.

Library Link 11: What is another popular southern treat that uses pecans?

BIBLIOGRAPHY—THE SOUTHEAST

Nonfiction

Anderson, Joan. *Pioneer Children of Appalachia*. Photographs by George Ancona. New York: Clarion Books, 1986. Grades 2 and up.
Photographs of Fort New Salem in Salem, West Virginia, a living history museum, recreate the lifestyle of a family that might have lived during the early 1800s.

Fox, Julian. *Tobacco*. East Sussex, U.K.: Wayland Publishers Limited, 1980. Grades 4 and up.
Using text and black-and-white photographs, Fox describes the cultivation, harvesting, and manufacture of tobacco in the South and throughout the world.

Krementz, Jill. *Sweet Pea: A Black Girl Growing Up in Rural South*. New York: Harcourt Brace and World, 1969. Grades 2 and up.
Sweet Pea's life of poverty is shown through black-and-white photographs of her as she goes to school, church, and her grandfather's farm.

Miles, Lewis. *Cotton*. East Sussex, U.K.: Wayland Publishers Limited, 1980. Grades 4 and up.
Cotton is important throughout the world, particularly in the southern United States. The cotton industry's development and its relationship to the textile industry is described.

Mitchell, Barbara. *A Pocketful of Goobers: A Story about George Washington Carver*. Illustrated by Peter E. Hanson. Minneapolis, Minn.: Carolrhoda Books, 1986. Grades 3 and up.
When the boll weevil hit the South in the early 1900s, Carver devoted his talents for growing to the peanut, developing many products still in demand today.

O'Kelley, Mattie Lou. *From the Hills of Georgia: An Autobiography in Paintings*. Boston: Little, Brown and Company, Inc., 1983. All ages.
O'Kelley's rich folk paintings and simple narrative tell the story of her youth in Georgia.

Phelan, Mary Kay. *The Story of the Louisiana Purchase*. Illustrated by Frank Aloise. New York: Thomas Y. Crowell, 1977. Grades 4 and up.
The acquisition of the Province of Louisiana in 1803 doubled the size of the young United States. Phelan uses a variety of accounts to tell the stories of the negotiations behind this purchase and of the people of the territory.

Selsam, Millicent E. *Peanut*. Photographs by Jerome Wexler. New York: William Morrow and Company, 1969. All ages.
The development of the peanut from seed to harvest is explored in color and black-and-white photographs. This is a simple yet thorough text.

Tunis, Edwin. *Shaw's Fortune: The Picture Story of a Colonial Plantation*. New York: Thomas Y. Crowell, 1966. Grades 4 and up.
Detailed line drawings enhance this recreation of the Shaw family's plantation in Virginia.

Fiction

Altsheler, Joseph A. *Kentucky Frontiermen*. Illustrated by Todd Doney. Nashville, Tenn.: Voyageur Publishing Inc., 1988. Grades 4 and up.
   Originally published in 1906 as *The Young Trailers*, this revised and updated version tells of the challenges of settling in Kentucky.

Armstrong, William H. *Sounder*. Illustrated by James Barkley. New York: Harper and Row, 1969. Grades 4 and up.
   Sounder is a faithful coon dog whose master is driven to theft to save his family. The master's imprisonment leaves the family to struggle for survival.

Beatty, Patricia. *Be Ever Hopeful, Hannalee*. New York: Morrow Junior Books, 1988. Grades 5 and up.
   The Civil War is finally over, and instead of returning home to stay, Hannalee must join her brother in Atlanta, where she faces hard work and danger.

Burch, Robert. *Christmas With Ida Early*. New York: Viking Penguin Inc., 1983. Grades 4 and up.
   Ida Early returns to the Sutton family for Christmas and makes the new preacher's Christmas pageant truly unconventional.

_____. *Ida Early Comes over the Mountain*. New York: Viking Penguin Inc., 1980. Grades 4 and up.
   Ida is unusual in dress and actions, but she brings happiness to the Suttons. When the children allow others to ridicule her, she loses her spirit, eventually leaving the family. When she returns, she has returned to her zany, usual style.

_____. *Queenie Peavy*. Illustrated by Jerry Lazare. New York: Viking Press, 1966. Grades 4 and up.
   It was hard to be thirteen years old in the 1930s, but irrepressible Queenie had character, proved by her actions and her humorous approach to life.

Caudill, Rebecca. *Did You Carry the Flag Today, Charley?* Illustrated by Nancy Grossman. New York: Holt, Rinehart and Winston, 1966. Grades 2 and up.
   Charley, who lives in the Appalachian Mountains, starts school and wants to achieve the honor of carrying the flag. His mischievous nature makes it a difficult, but not impossible, goal.

Cleaver, Vera, and Bill Cleaver. *Where the Lilies Bloom*. Illustrated by Jim Spanfeller. Philadelphia: J. B. Lippincott, 1969. Grades 4 and up.
   Mary Call keeps the family together in the Great Smoky Mountains by tricking the landlord into signing over their house and land. When their father dies they sell plants and herbs for medicine and earn money to plant their crops.

Crofford, Emily. *Stories from the Blue Road*. Minneapolis, Minn.: Carolrhoda Books, 1982. Grades 3 and up.
   Five moving stories are told about an Arkansas farm family during the Great Depression.

Edwards, Pat. *Little John and Plutie*. Boston: Houghton Mifflin Company, 1988. Grades 4 and up.
   The best part of moving to grandmother's house was meeting Pluto, but Little John soon realized it wasn't easy to be friends with a black boy in the South.

Ellison, Lucile Watkins. *Butter on Both Sides*. Illustrated by Judith Gwyn Brown. New York: Charles Scribner's Sons, 1979. Grades 4 and up.

Ellison tells the story of a family living in rural Alabama during the early 1900s. Sequels are *The Tie That Binds* (1982) and *A Window to Look Through* (1981).

Fox, Paula. *The Slave Dancer*. Illustrated by Eros Keith. Scarsdale, N.Y.: Bradbury Press, 1973. Grades 4 and up.

In 1840, thirteen-year-old Jessie, who lives in New Orleans, is captured to play his fife to exercise the blacks on a slave ship. Though this is primarily about his time on the ship, it is an excellent introduction to the issue of slavery.

Hays, Wilma Pitchford. *Mary's Star: A Tale of Orphans in Virginia in 1781*. Illustrated by Lawrence Beall Smith. New York: Holt, Rinehart and Winston, 1968. Grades 4 and up.

When Mary and her brother learn that their father was killed in the Revolutionary War, they face the challenges of being penniless orphans and the need to keep Mary's colt, Star.

_____. *Siege! The Story of St. Augustine in 1702*. Illustrated by Peter Cox. New York: Coward McCann and Geoghegan, 1976. Grades 2 and up.

When it becomes apparent that the English are about to attack, the Spanish settlers withdraw to the fort while Juan's father sails to Havana for help.

Hiser, Berniece T. *The Adventure of Charlie and His Wheat-Straw Hat: A Memorat*. Illustrated by Mary Szilagyi. New York: Dodd, Mead and Company, 1989. All ages.

Charlie's dad had left to fight in the Civil War, leaving Charlie with the family in their Appalachian mountain home. When soldiers come to steal Squire McIntosh's animals, Charlie's treasured straw hat is almost lost. Based on a true incident.

Hurmence, Belinda. *A Girl Called Boy*. New York: Clarion Books, 1982. Grades 5 and up.

Boy (Blanche Overtha Yancy) gets lost in the mountains of North Carolina and stumbles into a cabin. She realizes she has slipped back into the 1850s amid slave catchers and plantation owners. Through this fantasy the reader learns about the slavery issues of the period.

Lenski, Lois. *Strawberry Girl*. Philadelphia: J. B. Lippincott, 1945. Grades 3 and up.

Birdie Boyer lives in Florida with her family, which raises strawberries. Lenski's Newbery Medal book provides insights into the life of this region.

Mitchell, Barbara. *Hush Puppies*. Illustrated by Cherie R. Wyman. Minneapolis, Minn.: Carolrhoda Books, 1983. Grades 1 and up.

Juba is a plantation cook in the old South when she learns how to quiet the dogs with her hush puppies.

Rawls, Wilson. *Where the Red Fern Grows*. Garden City, N.Y.: Doubleday and Company, Inc., 1961. Grades 5 and up.

In the Ozark mountains, a young boy earns money to buy a pair of coon hounds. The story is moving and memorable.

Smucker, Barbara. *Runaway to Freedom: A Story of the Underground Railway*. New York: Harper and Row, 1977. Grades 4 and up.

Julilly and Liza escape from a Mississippi plantation and make their way to Canada on the Underground Railway.

Taylor, Mildred. *Roll of Thunder, Hear My Cry*. New York: Dial Books, Inc., 1976. Grades 5 and up.

In this powerful novel Cassie is nine during the Great Depression, learning about the inequities of being black in the South.

Taylor, Theodore. *Teetoncey*. Illustrated by Richard Cuffari. Garden City, N.Y.: Doubleday and Company, Inc., 1974. Grades 5 and up.

Ben O'Neal wants to prove to the North Carolina coastal community that he is as brave as his father was. He helps rescue a young girl from a shipwreck and then struggles to learn about her and himself. Sequels are *Teetoncey and Ben O'Neal* (Avon, 1984) and *The Odyssey of Ben O'Neal* (Avon, 1984).

Wilkinson, Brenda. *Not Separate, Not Equal*. New York: Harper and Row, 1987. Grades 5 and up.

Malene is a seventeen-year-old adopted black girl in 1965 and is one of the first six students to integrate the white high school in Pineridge, Georgia.

9
The Midwest and Prairies

Midwest and prairie states:
- Illinois
- Indiana
- Iowa
- Kansas
- Michigan
- Minnesota
- Missouri
- Nebraska
- North Dakota
- Ohio
- Oklahoma
- South Dakota
- Wisconsin

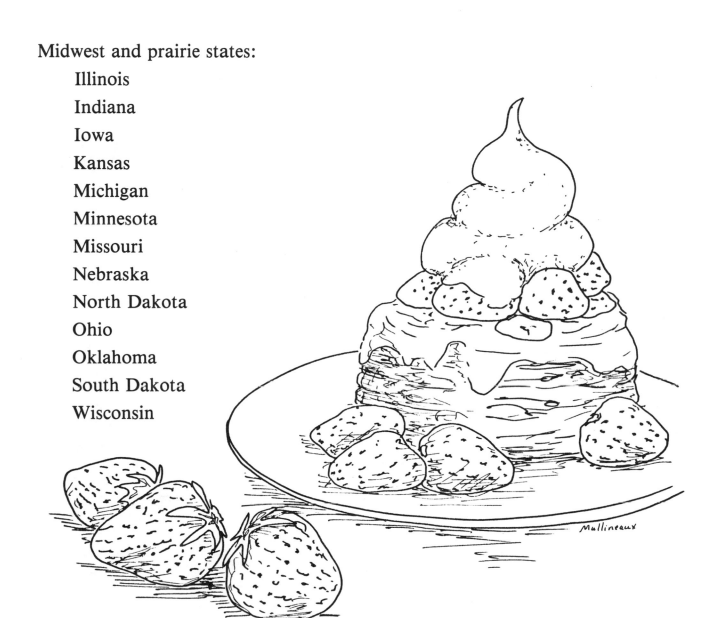

Chapter Nine
Word List

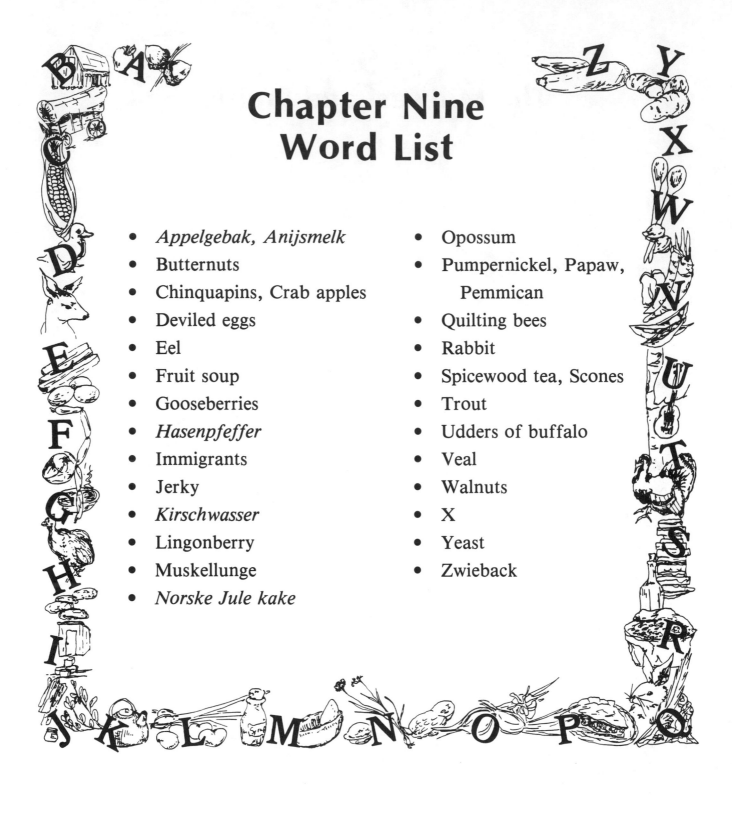

- *Appelgebak, Anijsmelk*
- Butternuts
- Chinquapins, Crab apples
- Deviled eggs
- Eel
- Fruit soup
- Gooseberries
- *Hasenpfeffer*
- Immigrants
- Jerky
- *Kirschwasser*
- Lingonberry
- Muskellunge
- *Norske Jule kake*
- Opossum
- Pumpernickel, Papaw, Pemmican
- Quilting bees
- Rabbit
- Spicewood tea, Scones
- Trout
- Udders of buffalo
- Veal
- Walnuts
- X
- Yeast
- Zwieback

CINNAMON ROLLS

Ingredients

2 packages dry yeast
¼ cup very warm water (110 to 115 degrees)
1¼ cups sugar
1 cup milk
3 tablespoons shortening
¾ teaspoon salt
1 egg, beaten

2 teaspoons vanilla
3 to 3½ cups flour
3 tablespoons melted butter
1½ teaspoons cinnamon
2 cups confectioner's sugar
1 tablespoon butter, softened
4 tablespoons milk

Steps

1. Dissolve yeast in warm water.
2. Add 1 teaspoon of the sugar.
3. Stir well.
4. Let yeast mixture stand.
5. Scald milk in medium saucepan.
6. Stir in shortening, salt, and ½ cup sugar.
7. Let mixture cool.
8. Stir in egg and vanilla.
9. Put 3 cups flour in a large bowl.
10. Add yeast mixture.
11. Add milk mixture.
12. Stir well until it forms a soft dough.
13. Put dough onto a floured board.
14. Knead for 10 minutes. Add more flour if dough is too sticky.
15. Grease a large bowl.
16. Put dough in bowl and roll it around to grease it.
17. Cover bowl with plastic wrap and let rise in a warm place until doubled in size (about 1 hour).
18. Punch dough. Roll out on a floured board to ¼-inch thickness.
19. Brush dough with melted butter.
20. Mix remaining sugar with cinnamon and sprinkle over buttered dough.
21. Roll dough up.
22. Using a sharp knife, cut slices 1 to 1½ inches thick.
23. Put slices down flat on a greased baking sheet.
24. Cover with a towel and let rise in a warm place until doubled in size (about 45 minutes).
25. Bake at 325 degrees for 20 to 25 minutes or until slightly brown.
26. Beat confectioner's sugar in a medium bowl with softened butter and milk to make frosting.
27. While rolls are still warm, frost with confectioner's frosting.

Makes 9 to 12.

Library Link 1: Where does cinnamon come from?

SWISS FONDUE

Ingredients
1 cup milk
¼ cup soft bread crumbs
½ pound Swiss cheese
1 tablespoon butter
½ teaspoon salt
3 eggs
French bread, cut in cubes

Steps
1. Mix milk, bread crumbs, cheese, butter, and salt in a large saucepan.
2. Cook over low heat until smooth, stirring constantly.
3. Remove from heat.
4. Separate egg yolks from egg whites.
5. Beat egg yolks.
6. Stir egg yolks into cheese mixture.
7. Beat egg whites until stiff.
8. Fold egg whites carefully into cheese mixture.
9. Pour mixture in a fondue pot. (Mixture may be reheated by baking in the oven.)
10. Dip chunks of bread into the fondue to serve.

Serves 4.

Library Link 2: According to tradition, what happens if a girl drops a chunk of bread into the fondue?

CHICAGO DEEP-DISH PIZZA

Ingredients
1 package dry yeast
1 teaspoon sugar
1 cup very warm water (110 to 115 degrees)
3 cups flour
½ cup cornmeal
1 teaspoon salt
¼ cup salad oil
1 pound shredded mozarella cheese
1 pound Italian sausage
1 28-ounce can pizza sauce
½ teaspoon Italian seasoning
4 tablespoons grated Parmesan cheese

Steps
1. Dissolve yeast in ¼ cup water.
2. Add sugar and stir well. Set aside.
3. In a large bowl combine 2½ cups flour, cornmeal, salt, oil, and remaining ¾ cup water. Stir well.
4. Stir in yeast mixture.
5. Put dough onto a floured board. Let rest 5 minutes.
6. Knead dough 10 minutes. Add the rest of the flour as needed.
7. Grease a large bowl.
8. Put dough in bowl and roll it around until it is greased.
9. Cover with plastic wrap and let rise in a warm place until doubled in size (1 to 2 hours).
10. Preheat oven to 475 degrees.
11. Punch dough down.
12. Oil a deep-dish pizza pan or a 12-by-15-inch cake pan.
13. Press dough out to cover the bottom of the pan.
14. Let dough rise in a warm place for 30 minutes.
15. Cook and drain Italian sausage.
16. Spread pizza sauce over dough.
17. Sprinkle Italian seasoning, sausage, and shredded mozarella cheese over sauce.
18. Sprinkle Parmesan cheese on top.
19. Bake 15 minutes.
20. Lower oven temperature to 375 degrees and bake 20 to 30 minutes more. Bottom of crust should be browned.

Serves 4.

Library Link 3: After the Civil War, Chicago became the most important meat marketing center in the world. What invention made mass production of meat possible?

PASTIES

Ingredients
4 cups flour
½ teaspoon salt
1⅔ cups shortening, softened
1 cup cold water
1 large potato
2 carrots
1 small onion
½ pound ground beef
½ pound ground pork
2 tablespoons dried parsley
1 teaspoon salt
¼ teaspoon pepper
2 tablespoons melted butter

Steps
1. Combine flour and salt in a large bowl.
2. Cut in the shortening with knives until it is crumbly.
3. Slowly stir in the water until dough forms a sticky ball.
4. Flour a sheet of waxed paper. Roll dough in a ball and wrap it in the waxed paper.
5. Put dough in refrigerator for 1 hour.
6. Peel potato and chop into fine pieces. Put it in a large bowl.
7. Peel carrots and chop into fine pieces. Add carrots to the potatoes.
8. Peel and chop the onion. Add onion to the potatoes and carrots.
9. Add ground beef, ground pork, parsley, salt, pepper, and melted butter to the potato mixture. Mix well.
10. Preheat oven to 350 degrees.
11. Divide dough into 4 to 6 equal parts, depending on the size of pasty you want.
12. Roll each piece out onto a floured board to make a 6 to 9 inch circle.
13. Divide potato mixture evenly among the dough circles.
14. Place mixture in middle of each circle.
15. Fold circles in half, forming a half moon shape. Press edges together.
16. Crimp sealed edges with a fork.
17. Put pasties on a greased cookie sheet.
18. Bake 1 hour and 15 minutes to 1 hour and 25 minutes or until browned and cooked through.

Makes 4 to 6.

Library Link 4:   Where did pasties originate?

CONEYS

Ingredients

1 pound ground beef
1 small onion, chopped
1 tablespoon mustard
2 tablespoons vinegar
2 tablespoons sugar
1 tablespoon water
½ teaspoon Worcestershire sauce

¼ teaspoon salt
¼ teaspoon Tabasco sauce
Ketchup
6 hot dogs
6 hot dog rolls
Shredded cheddar cheese,
    if desired

Steps

1. Crumble and cook ground beef in a large skillet over medium heat.
2. Add onion and cook until clear and soft.
3. Add mustard, vinegar, sugar, water, Worcestershire sauce, salt, and Tabasco sauce. Stir well.
4. Simmer meat mixture over low heat.
5. Add enough ketchup to flavor.
6. Simmer 1 hour.
7. Cook hot dogs in boiling water until done (about 10 minutes).
8. Put hot dogs in rolls and top with meat sauce. Add cheddar cheese if desired.

Serves 6.

Library Link 5: How did frankfurters become known as hot dogs?

FISH BALLS

Ingredients

½ pound cod
2½ cups potatoes, peeled and cubed
1 tablespoon butter
1 beaten egg

¼ teaspoon pepper
¼ teaspoon salt
Butter for frying

Steps

1. Put fish and potatoes in a large saucepan and cover with water.
2. Boil until potatoes are almost soft.
3. Drain until nearly dry.
4. Mash mixture together
5. Stir in butter, egg, pepper, and salt.
6. Beat until mixture is smooth.
7. Heat butter in large frying pan.
8. Form fish mixture into balls and fry in butter until well browned on all sides.

Serves 6.

Library Link 6: Cod are saltwater fish. What fish are both saltwater and freshwater fish?

ANGEL FOOD CAKE

Ingredients

10 egg whites,
    at room temperature
¼ teaspoon salt
1 teaspoon cream of tartar

½ teaspoon almond extract
1 teaspoon vanilla extract
1½ cups sugar
1 cup flour

Steps

1. Put the egg whites and salt in a large metal or glass bowl.
2. Beat with an electric mixer on high until foamy.
3. Add cream of tartar and beat until soft peaks form.
4. Add almond and vanilla extracts. Mix well.
5. Mix flour and sugar together in a small bowl.
6. Add 2 tablespoons of the flour mixture to the egg whites. Fold in carefully using a wire whisk.
7. Continue to fold in flour mixture 2 tablespoons at a time until it is all mixed in.
8. Preheat oven to 325 degrees.
9. Pour batter into a 10-inch, ungreased tube pan.
10. Bake for 50 minutes. Turn the oven off and leave cake in the oven for 10 more minutes.
11. Remove pan from oven. Turn upside down until the cake cools.

Makes 1 cake.

Library Link 7: Where was angel food cake first created?

STRAWBERRY SHORTCAKE

Ingredients

1 pint fresh strawberries
⅓ cup sugar, or to taste
1 cup flour
2 teaspoons baking powder
¼ teaspoon salt

1 tablespoon sugar
4 tablespoons shortening
¼ cup milk
Heavy cream

Steps

1. Hull and wash berries.
2. Put berries in a medium-sized bowl. Chop into large pieces.
3. Add sugar to taste. Stir well.
4. Set berry mixture aside.
5. Put flour, baking powder, salt, and sugar into a large bowl. Stir.
6. Cut the shortening into the flour mixture until crumbly.
7. Add milk. Stir to make a stiff dough. Add milk if it becomes too dry.
8. Pat dough onto a floured board to ¾-inch thickness.
9. Cut dough with a round cutter. Place on an ungreased baking sheet.
10. Bake at 400 degrees for about 15 minutes or until browned.
11. Split and butter warm shortcakes.
12. Spoon berries over shortcakes. Top with heavy cream.

Serves 4 to 5.

Library Link 8: What did the early settlers call strawberry shortcake?

DUTCH APPLE KUCHEN

Ingredients

2 cups flour
4 teaspoons baking powder
½ teaspoon salt
⅓ cup sugar
⅓ cup softened butter
1 egg

⅓ cup milk
5 sour apples
½ cup sugar
1 teaspoon cinnamon
3 tablespoons currants
Whipped cream

Steps

1. Stir together flour, baking powder, salt, and ⅓ cup sugar in a large mixing bowl.
2. Mix in butter and egg until mixture is crumbly.
3. Stir in milk until dough holds together.
4. Grease a 9-inch round cake pan.
5. Spread dough in pan.
6. Preheat oven to 350 degrees.
7. Peel, core, and slice apples.
8. Arrange apples in a pattern on top of the dough.
9. Mix ½ cup sugar and cinnamon.
10. Sprinkle sugar and cinnamon mixture over apples.
11. Sprinkle currants over apples.
12. Bake 25 to 30 minutes or until apples are tender and cake is done.
13. Serve with whipped cream on top.

Makes 1 cake.

Library Link 9:   How did Johnny Appleseed obtain his seeds?

SPRITZ COOKIES

Ingredients

1 cup softened butter
¾ cup sugar
1 egg
2¼ cups flour

½ teaspoon baking powder
¼ teaspoon salt
1 teaspoon vanilla extract

Steps

1. Cream shortening in a large mixing bowl.
2. Stir in sugar and egg. Mix well.
3. Add flour, baking powder, salt, and vanilla. Mix well.
4. Force dough through a cookie press onto an ungreased cookie sheet.
5. Bake at 375 degrees for 8 to 12 minutes or until cookies are slightly brown on the bottom.

Makes 4½ to 5 dozen.

Library Link 10:   Where does the name *Spritz* come from and what does it mean?

BIBLIOGRAPHY—THE MIDWEST AND PRAIRIES

Nonfiction

Conrad, Pam. *Prairie Songs*. Illustrated by Darryl S. Zudeck. New York: Harper and Row, 1985. Grades 5 and up.
A Nebraska prairie winter is long and difficult. A young child tells of the hardships faced and the comfort found with the family during one winter.

Engel, Lorenz. *Among the Plains Indians*. Minneapolis, Minn.: Lerner Publications Company, 1972. Grades 3 and up.
The lithographs of George Catlin and the engravings of Karl Bodmer illustrate this book about the Plains Indians. The text is straightforward and easily read.

Glubok, Shirley. *The Art of the Plains Indians*. Photographs by Alfred Tamarin. New York: Macmillan Publishing Company, Inc., 1975. Grades 3 and up.
A brief history of the Plains Indians is interspersed with illustrations and photographs of their art, clothing, tepees, decorations, weapons, and everyday utensils.

Henry, Joanne Landers. *Log Cabin in the Woods: A True Story about a Pioneer Boy*. Illustrated by Joyce Audy Zarins. New York: Four Winds Press, 1988. Grades 3 and up.
Oliver Johnson was eleven in 1832, the year of this true story about growing up as a pioneer child in Indiana.

Hirsch, S. Carl. *Famous American Indians of the Plains*. Illustrated by Lorence Bjorklund. Chicago: Rand McNally and Company, 1973. Grades 3 and up.
Line drawings and occasional color illustrations highlight stories of the nomadic life of the culture sometimes known as the "horse culture."

May, Robin. *Plains Indians of North America*. Vero Beach, Fla.: Rourke Publications, Inc., 1987. Grades 3 and up.
Color photographs illustrate this relatively simple discussion of the life of the Plains Indians.

_____. *Plains Indian Warrior*. Illustrated by Mark Bergin. Vero Beach, Fla.: Rourke Publications, Inc., 1988. Grades 2 and up.
May tells the story of the life of the Plains Indians in simple text. Prints and color illustrations are included.

McGovern, Ann. *...If You Lived with the Sioux Indians*. Illustrated by Bob Levering. New York: Four Winds Press, 1972. Grades 3 and up.
Line drawings, maps, and text answer questions of interest to young students researching Sioux Indians.

Rinkoff, Barbara. *Guess What Grasses Do*. Illustrated by Beatrice Darwin. New York: Lothrop Lee and Shepard Company, 1971. All ages.
Woodcuts and earth colors illustrate the importance of grasses in Indian and other cultures.

Simon, Charnan. *The Story of the Haymarket Riot*. Chicago: Childrens Press, 1988. Grades 3 and up.

In 1886 Union speakers in Chicago's Haymarket Square were calling for shorter working hours and higher pay. The ensuing riot prompted workers across the country to join in the demands. Simon's book describes the riot, trial, and the results.

Steele, William O. *Talking Bones: Secrets of Indian Burial Mounds*. Illustrated by Carlos Llerena-Aguirre. New York: Harper and Row, 1978. Grades 4 and up.

Indian burial mounds, primarily found in the eastern half of America, provide a fascinating glimpse into the customs and rituals of the prehistoric American Indians.

Stein, R. Conrad. *The Story of the Chicago Fire*. Illustrated by Richard Wahl. Chicago: Childrens Press, 1982. Grades 3 and up.

In 1871 Chicago was thriving. But the great fire changed the lives of everyone involved. Though some feared Chicago was dead, the city was quickly rebuilt.

_____. *The Story of the Homestead Act*. Illustrated by Cathy Koenig. Chicago: Childrens Press, 1978. Grades 3 and up.

Americans needed encouragement to settle in the Midwest, and the Homestead Act provided exactly the incentive needed: free land. Stein describes the challenges faced by those hardy Americans who were willing to work hard for their farmland.

Strait, Treva Adams. *The Price of Free Land*. New York: J. B. Lippincott, 1979. Grades 3 and up.

The land was free if the homesteaders would stay there three years. But the price was high. The winter on the Nebraska prairie, the tornadoes, and other challenges are described.

Watts, Franklin. *Wheat*. Illustrated by Sam Shiromani. Chicago: Childrens Press, 1977. All ages.

The importance of wheat is described with photographs and simple text.

Wilson, Terry P. *Indians of North America: The Osage*. New York: Chelsea House Publishers, 1988. Grades 4 and up.

The Osage occupied the Mississippi River Valley in the eighteenth century, and their skills were valued by French traders. Rich text and color and black-and-white photographs describe their transitions from the arrival of the settlers to the present.

Wood, Frances E. *Panoramic Plains: The Great Plains States*. Chicago: Childrens Press, 1962. Grades 4 and up.

From prehistoric to modern times, Wood discusses the exploration, settling, and development of the Plains states: Iowa, Kansas, Missouri, Nebraska, North Dakota, and South Dakota.

Yue, David, and Charlotte Yue. *The Tipi: A Center of Native American Life*. New York: Alfred A. Knopf, Inc., 1984. Grades 3 and up.

The structure, furnishings, and elements of the sophisticated dwelling of the Plains Indians known as the tipi (tepee) are described with text and line drawings.

Fiction

Brink, Carol Ryrie. *Caddie Woodlawn*. Illustrated by Trina Schart Hyman. New York: Macmillan Publishing Company, 1935. Grades 4 and up.

Eleven-year-old Caddie has many adventures while growing up on the Wisconsin frontier of the mid-1800s.

Brown, Irene Bennett. *Willow Whip*. New York: Atheneum, 1979. Grades 4 and up.
     Willow is desperate for her family to have their own farm. She pushes herself so hard that she is nicknamed "Willow the Whip" and nearly dies from sunstroke. Finally she realizes she must strike a balance between work and play.

Bulla, Clyde Robert. *Down the Mississippi*. New York: Thomas Y. Crowell, 1954. Grades 3 and up.
     Erik leaves his Minnesota farm and goes down the river on a log raft, encountering storms and an Indian raid.

Constant, Alberta Wilson. *Does Anybody Care about Lou Emma Miller?* New York: Harper and Row, 1979. Grades 5 and up.
     A young girl struggles with growing up in Kansas before World War I.

_____. *Those Miller Girls!* New York: Thomas Y. Crowell, 1965. Grades 5 and up.
     A college professor brings his motherless daughters to a new life in Kansas in the early 1900s.

Friermood, Elisabeth Hamilton. *Focus the Bright Land*. Garden City, N.Y.: Doubleday and Company, Inc., 1967. Grades 5 and up.
     Vicky lives in the Midwest in 1881. She is the only girl in a family of photographers, and one summer she convinces her family to let her join her two brothers traveling in a horse-drawn studio.

Harvey, Brett. *My Prairie Year: Based on the Diary of Elenore Plaisted*. Illustrated by Deborah Kogan Ray. New York: Holiday House, 1986. Grades 2 and up.
     Harvey draws upon her grandmother's journal of her days in the Dakota territory, beginning in 1889, to create a fascinating glimpse of early life.

Hurwitz, Johanna. *The Rabbi's Girls*. Illustrated by Pamela Johnson. New York: William Morrow and Company, 1982. Grades 4 and up.
     It is 1924, and the five Levin sisters are growing up in Ohio.

Kurelek, William. *A Prairie Boy's Summer*. Boston: Houghton Mifflin Company, 1975. Grades 2 and up.
     School may be out, but a prairie boy has work ahead: milking cows, plowing, haying, and so forth.

_____. *Prairie Boy's Winter*. Boston: Houghton Mifflin Company, 1973. Grades 2 and up.
     Winters were difficult, but there was also fun for William's family: playing ice hockey, making snow tunnels and forts, and skating on bog ditches.

MacLachlan, Patricia. *Sarah, Plain and Tall*. New York: Harper and Row, 1985. Grades 2 and up.
     Sarah is a mail-order bride who wins the love of two frontier children in this Newbery Medal book.

Miles, Betty. *I Would if I Could*. New York: Alfred A. Knopf, Inc., 1982. Grades 3 and up.
     It is summer in 1930, and a ten-year-old girl is visiting her grandmother in rural Ohio.

Monjo, F. N. *Willie Jasper's Golden Eagle*. Illustrated by Douglas Gorsline. Garden City, N.Y.: Doubleday and Company, Inc., 1976. Grades 3 and up.
     It is the late 1860s, and when Willie wins a spelling bee his father takes him on a trip on the steamboat *Natchez* down the Mississippi River. He witnesses the race between the *Natchez* and the *Robert E. Lee* from St. Louis to New Orleans.

Olsen, Violet. *The Growing Season*. New York: Atheneum, 1982. Grades 5 and up.
Life is difficult for Marie, who is living on an Iowa farm during the Great Depression.

Potter, Marian. *A Chance Wild Apple*. New York: William Morrow and Company, 1982. Grades 5 and up.
A young girl describes her life on a Missouri farm during the Great Depression.

Purdy, Carol. *Iva Dunnit and the Big Wind*. Illustrated by Steven Kellogg. New York: Dial Books, Inc., 1985. All ages.
In this tall tale, Iva Dunnit and her six children survive winds, wolves, and fires on the prairie.

Talbot, Charlene Joy. *An Orphan for Nebraska*. New York: Atheneum, 1979. Grades 4 and up.
It is the 1870s, and an orphaned Irish immigrant boy is sent to Nebraska.

Taylor, Theodore. *Walking up a Rainbow*. New York: Delacorte Press, 1986. Grades 6 and up.
Susan is an orphan in Iowa left with two thousand sheep and a huge debt. To save her home she starts a wagon train to Sacramento to sell her sheep.

Turner, Ann. *Dakota Dugout*. New York: Macmillan Publishing Company, Inc., 1985. Grades 1 and up.
Life in a sod house is described, including the killing winter, the summer drought, and the unending isolation. Finally the family's existence improves, but the early years are remembered fondly.

Wiegand, Roberta. *The Year of the Comet*. Scarsdale, N.Y.: Bradbury Press, 1984. Grades 5 and up.
A young girl is growing up in Nebraska during the 1900s.

Wilder, Laura Ingalls. *Little House in the Big Woods*. Illustrated by Garth Williams. New York: Harper and Row, 1953. Grades 3 and up.
This is one of a series of stories about life on the prairie. See also: *Little House on the Prairie, On the Banks of Plum Creek, By the Shores of Silver Lake, Farmer Boy, The Long Winter, Little Town on the Prairie*, and *These Happy Golden Years*, all published by Harper and Row in 1953.

10
The Southwest

Southwest states:

Texas

New Mexico

Arizona

Chapter Ten
Word List

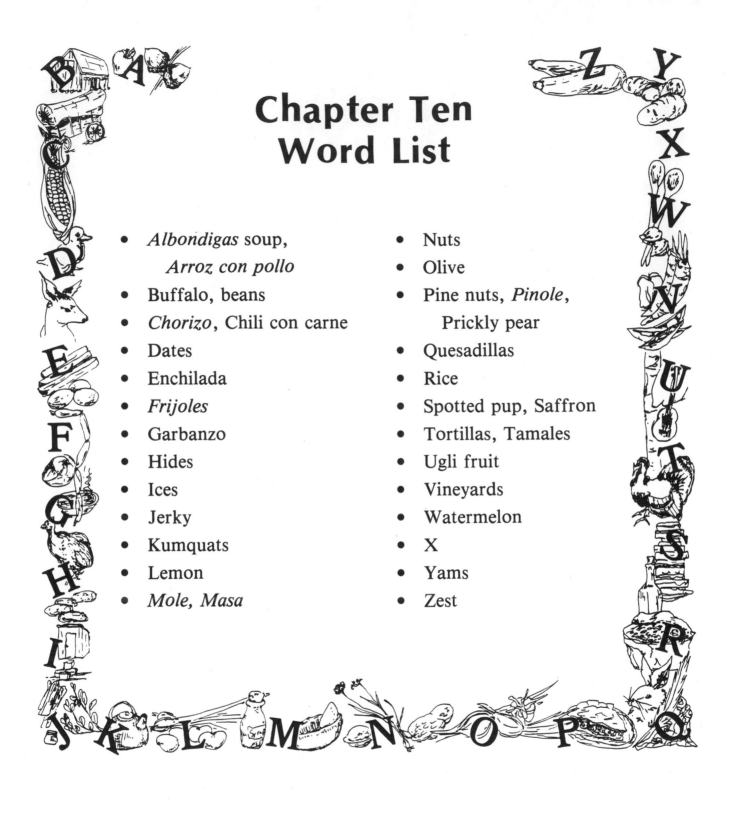

- *Albondigas* soup, *Arroz con pollo*
- Buffalo, beans
- *Chorizo*, Chili con carne
- Dates
- Enchilada
- *Frijoles*
- Garbanzo
- Hides
- Ices
- Jerky
- Kumquats
- Lemon
- *Mole, Masa*
- Nuts
- Olive
- Pine nuts, *Pinole*, Prickly pear
- Quesadillas
- Rice
- Spotted pup, Saffron
- Tortillas, Tamales
- Ugli fruit
- Vineyards
- Watermelon
- X
- Yams
- Zest

TORTILLAS

Ingredients

2 cups flour
1 teaspoon baking powder
2 teaspoons salt

2 tablespoons shortening, softened
½ cup water

Steps

1. Mix flour, baking powder, and salt in a large mixing bowl.
2. Cut in shortening.
3. Add water. Mix into a smooth dough with hands.
4. Let dough rest for 15 minutes in a covered bowl.
5. Pinch off a small piece of dough.
6. Roll dough into a small, thin circle.
7. Heat an ungreased frying pan over medium heat.
8. Put a circle of dough into the frying pan.
9. Cook until light brown on both sides.

Makes 8 to 10.

Library Link 1: What two grains are tortillas commonly made from?

BURRITOS

Ingredients

1½ pounds cooked pork,
    cut into small pieces
3 small cans chicken broth
2 7-ounce cans green chilis,
    chopped
1 16-ounce can tomatoes, chopped
12 tortillas (see previous recipe)

2 16-ounce cans refried beans
    (or see following recipe)
4 tablespoons cornstarch
⅓ cup water
2½ cups grated cheddar cheese
3 tomatoes, chopped
2½ cups shredded lettuce

Steps

1. Put pork in a medium saucepan. Add chicken broth.
2. Cook over medium heat for 10 minutes.
3. Add chilis and canned tomatoes. Cook for 15 minutes. This is green chili.
4. Remove from heat.
5. Spread each tortilla with refried beans.
6. Strain green chili with a slotted spoon. Spread over refried beans.
7. Roll each tortilla up. Place in a 9-by-13-inch baking pan.
8. Bake uncovered at 350 degrees for 10 minutes or until hot.
9. Mix cornstarch and ⅓ cup water in a small bowl.
10. Bring remaining green chili to a boil again over medium-high heat.
11. Slowly pour cornstarch mixture into chicken broth. Stir constantly until thickened.
12. Spoon green chili over burritos.
13. Sprinkle cheese, lettuce, and tomatoes over burritos.
14. Serve hot.

Serves 6.

Library Link 2: What Indian tribes lived in the southwest?

REFRIED BEANS

Ingredients
1 pound dried pinto beans (2 cups)
1 small onion, diced
1 clove garlic, minced
½ pound salt pork or bacon, diced
1 teaspoon cumin
Salt and pepper to taste
Monterey Jack cheese, shredded

Steps
1. Place beans in a large saucepan. Cover with water.
2. Bring to a boil. Boil 5 minutes.
3. Remove from heat. Cover and let beans sit for 1 hour.
4. Drain beans.
5. Put beans back in pan. Cover with water again.
6. Add onion, garlic, half of the pork, and cumin.
7. Bring to a boil. Boil until beans are tender (about 3 hours), adding water when needed to keep beans from drying.
8. Fry rest of pork until crisp in a large frying pan over medium heat.
9. Add beans to frying pan a little at a time, mashing as you add them.
10. Keep adding and mashing beans until they are the desired consistency.
11. Remove from heat and stir in salt and pepper to taste.
12. May be served warm with cheese sprinkled on top. Or, use in other recipes.

Serves 6 to 8.

Library Link 3:   Name as many kinds of beans as you can.

CHILI CON CARNE

Ingredients
1 pound ground beef
1 medium onion, chopped fine
1 clove garlic, chopped fine
2 small cans stewed tomatoes
2 small cans chili beans in chili sauce
1 teaspoon salt
½ teaspoon pepper
1½ teaspoons chili powder

Steps
1. In a large, deep skillet, fry ground beef over medium-high heat until browned and crumbly. Drain off grease.
2. Add onion and garlic. Cook until clear and soft.
3. Stir in tomatoes, chili beans, salt, pepper, and chili powder.
4. Simmer over low heat 45 minutes to 1 hour. Stir occasionally.

Serves 4 to 6.

Library Link 4:   What is the origin of chili con carne?

TAMALE PIE

Ingredients

2 cups cornmeal
Water
2 pounds ground beef
1 clove garlic, chopped fine
¼ teaspoon oregano, crushed
1 tablespoon flour
1½ cups water
1½ cups pitted, ripe olives, chopped fine
1 large can stewed tomatoes
1 tablespoon red chili powder
2 cups Longhorn cheddar cheese, grated
1 cup Monterey Jack cheese, grated

Steps

1. Put cornmeal in a large saucepan. Cover with water.
2. Cook over medium heat, adding water when necessary, until cornmeal makes a thick mush (about ½ hour).
3. Put ground beef, garlic, and oregano in a large frying pan. Cook over medium heat until beef is cooked through.
4. Stir flour into the beef mixture. Mix well.
5. Add 1½ cups water to make a gravy. Stir well.
6. Stir in olives, tomatoes, and red chili powder. Simmer 15 minutes.
7. Add 1 cup Longhorn cheddar cheese to cooked mush. Stir.
8. Pour mush into a large casserole or 9-by-13-inch baking pan.
9. Layer the Monterey Jack cheese and ground beef in the pan until both are used up (2 to 3 layers of each), ending with cheese on top.
10. Bake at 350 degrees for 1 hour.

Serves 6 to 8.

Library Link 5: What are regular tamales wrapped in?

TRAPPERS FRUIT

Ingredients

2 pounds dried apples
4 tablespoons honey
½ cup raisins
2 cups applesauce
⅓ cup chopped nuts
¼ cup cider

Steps

1. Put all ingredients in a large saucepan.
2. Cook over medium-low heat for 15 to 20 minutes. Stir often.
3. Remove from heat. Let cool before eating.

Serves 6 to 8.

Library Link 6: What is applejack?

CAPIROTADA

Ingredients

1 cup raisins
1 cup hot water
4 eggs
2 cups milk
½ pound brown sugar
1½ cups sliced apples

1½ teaspoons cinnamon
1 teaspoon nutmeg
3 slices dried or toasted bread
1 stick butter, melted
1 cup Longhorn cheddar cheese, grated

Steps

1. Put raisins in a small bowl and pour hot water over them.
2. Let sit for 5 minutes. Drain.
3. Put eggs in a large bowl. Beat well.
4. Add milk. Stir.
5. Add brown sugar. Mix well.
6. Stir in apples, cinnamon, and nutmeg.
7. Tear bread into small pieces. Add to milk and egg mixture.
8. Stir in melted butter.
9. Add raisins. Mix well.
10. Pour ½ of the egg mixture into a 1½- to 2-quart casserole dish.
11. Sprinkle ½ of the cheese over it.
12. Pour the rest of the milk mixture into the casserole dish.
13. Sprinkle the rest of the cheese on top of it.
14. Bake at 350 degrees 45 minutes or until done in the middle.

Serves 4.

Library Link 7: Why did the Spanish call this dessert "spotted dog"?

WO-JAPI

Ingredients

1 large (20-ounce) can blackberries
2 cups sugar
3 tablespoons flour

Water
1 teaspoon lemon juice

Steps

1. Drain blackberries. Save the juice.
2. Put blackberries and sugar in a medium saucepan.
3. Measure juice from blackberries. Add water to equal 2 cups.
4. Mix flour, juice, and water in a small bowl. Mix thoroughly.
5. Add flour mixture to berries and sugar.
6. Cook over medium-high heat until mixture boils. Stir frequently.
7. Turn heat down. Simmer slowly for 15 minutes.
8. Stir in lemon juice.
9. Chill before serving.

Serves 4 to 6.

Library Link 8: What Indian tribe favored this dessert?

BISCOCHITOS

Ingredients

3 eggs
1 cup shortening, softened
2 cups flour
1¾ cups sugar

2 tablespoons anise seed
2 tablespoons vanilla
4 tablespoons water
Cinnamon

Steps

1. Beat eggs well in a small bowl.
2. Cut in shortening with flour in a large bowl.
3. Mix sugar into flour and shortening.
4. Add eggs and anise seeds. Mix well.
5. Make mixture into a firm dough. Add more flour if needed.
6. Roll dough out onto a floured board about ½ inch thick.
7. Cut dough with cookie cutters. Place on cookie sheet.
8. Mix vanilla with water.
9. Brush vanilla mixture on tops of cookie. Sprinkle with cinnamon.
10. Bake at 375 degrees for 3 to 5 minutes or until slightly brown.
11. Serve warm.

Makes 3 to 4 dozen.

Library Link 9: This traditional cookie is used for what holiday in what state?

SOPAIPILLAS

Ingredients

4 cups flour
2½ teaspoons baking powder
2 teaspoons salt
1 tablespoon shortening, softened

1¼ cups water
Oil for deep fat frying
Honey

Steps

1. Mix flour, baking powder, and salt in a large mixing bowl.
2. Cut in shortening.
3. Add water and knead with hands until dough is smooth.
4. Put dough in a plastic bag and let stand for 2 hours.
5. Roll dough out very thin on a floured board.
6. Cut dough into small triangles.
7. Heat oil in a large saucepan to 375 degrees.
8. Drop triangles into hot oil. Fry until browned on both sides.
9. Drain triangles on paper towels.
10. Serve warm with honey.

Serves 10.

Library Link 10: Barbecues originated in the Southwest. What is the origin and meaning of the word *barbecue*?

PINOLE

Ingredients
1 cup cornmeal
⅓ cup sugar
½ teaspoon cinnamon
¼ teaspoon nutmeg
3 cups milk

Steps
1. Spread cornmeal on a cookie sheet.
2. Bake at 425 degrees for 5 minutes, stirring every two minutes.
3. Remove from oven. Cool.
4. Mix sugar, cinnamon, and nutmeg together.
5. Add sugar mixture to cornmeal. Mix well.
6. Pour cornmeal mixture into a large saucepan.
7. Stir milk in slowly.
8. Cook over medium heat for 15 minutes, stirring constantly, or until mixture is thickened.

Serves 4.

Library Link 11: This beverage is a combination of what two cultures?

BIBLIOGRAPHY—THE SOUTHWEST

Nonfiction

Ashabranner, Brent. *Born to the Land: An American Portrait*. Photographs by Paul Conklin. New York: G. P. Putnam's Sons, 1989. Grades 4 and up.
   Though primarily about present-day New Mexico, this story begins with pioneer days, providing insights into the challenges faced by any rural community.

Baker, Betty. *At the Center of the World*. Illustrated by Murray Tinkelman. New York: Macmillan Publishing Company, Inc., 1973. Grades 3 and up.
   Baker retells the creation myth of the Pima and Papago tribes of southern Arizona and northern Mexico. Line drawings highlight this beautiful story.

Baylor, Byrd. *When Clay Sings*. Illustrated by Tom Bahti. New York: Charles Scribner's Sons, 1972. All ages.
   The Indian desert pottery tells a story, and Baylor's poetry with Bahti's drawings help the reader understand this important aspect of Indian life.

Colby, C. B. *Cliff Dwellings: Ancient Ruins from America's Past*. New York: Coward McCann and Geoghegan, 1965. Grades 4 and up.
   Ruins from New Mexico, Arizona, Utah, and Colorado are described with black-and-white photographs, maps, and text.

_____. *Settlers and Strangers: Native Americans of the Desert Southwest and History as They Saw It*. New York: Macmillan Publishing Company, Inc., 1977. Grades 4 and up.
The story of the Native Americans of the Southwest began long before the new Americans settled in the Southwest. History, myths, customs, art, and religion are woven together with black-and-white photos to tell the story.

Place, Marian T. *The First Book of the Santa Fe Trail*. Illustrated by Paul Frame. New York: Franklin Watts, Inc., 1966. Grades 4 and up.
The story of the Santa Fe Trail began in 1806, when Congress sent Lieutenant Zebulon M. Pike to explore the southern boundary of the Louisiana Purchase. When he stumbled into Spanish territory, he was arrested and taken to Santa Fe.

Radlauer, Ed. *Mesa Verde, National Park*. Chicago: Childrens Press, 1984. Grades 2 and up.
Colorful photographs and simple text tell the story of Mesa Verde. This is a good first book.

Robinson, Maudie. *Children of the Sun: The Pueblos, Navajos, and Apaches of New Mexico*. New York: Simon and Schuster, 1973. Grades 3 and up.
The religion, customs, songs, stories, and crafts of the Southwest Indians are described. Photographs are especially effective, especially those of rugs, pottery, and jewelry.

Siebert, Diane. *Mojave*. Illustrated by Wendell Minor. New York: Thomas Y. Crowell, 1988. All ages.
Siebert's tumbleweeds are stumbling and bumbling, and Minor's paintings are stunning in this magnificent portrayal of the desert.

Tamarin, Alfred, and Shirley Glubok. *Ancient Indians of the Southwest*. Garden City, N.Y.: Doubleday and Company, Inc., 1975. Grades 4 and up.
Chapters are included on a variety of relatively unfamiliar Indian tribes: the Mogollon, Hohokam, Sinagua, Salado Cohonina, Patayan, and Anasazi. Black-and-white photographs are plentiful.

Wolf, Bernard. *Tinker and the Medicine Men: The Story of a Navajo Boy of Monument Valley*. New York: Random House, 1973. Grades 2 and up.
Tinker, a Navaho boy, wants to be a medicine man. When school ends he returns to Monument Valley, Arizona. Life lessons, culture, and customs are described through photos and text.

Wood, Nancy. *Hollering Sun*. Photos by Myron Wood. New York: Simon and Schuster, 1972. All ages.
Photos, poetry, and prose describe the past and present philosophy and legends of the Indians of Taos Pueblo.

Young, Donald. *The Great American Desert*. New York: Julian Messner, 1980. Grades 3 and up.
Young's photographs and text describe the making of the desert, the plant life, the animals, exploring the desert, and places to visit.

Fiction

Armer, Laura Adams. *Waterless Mountain*. Illustrated by Sidney Armer and Laura Adams Armer. New York: David McKay Company, Inc., 1931. Grades 4 and up.
This story of a Navajo Indian boy's training in the ancient religion of his people is set against the deserts of northern Arizona.

Baylor, Byrd. *Desert Voices*. Illustrated by Peter Parnall. New York: Charles Scribner's Sons, 1981. All ages.

Through poetic lines and colorful line drawings, ten desert animals tell of their lives and their beloved desert homes.

_____. *Your Own Best Secret Place*. Illustrated by Peter Parnall. New York: Charles Scribner's Sons, 1979. All ages.

Baylor writes in poetic style about the secret place she found, formerly visited by William Cottonwood. The beauty of the Southwest desert is evoked with Parnall's drawings.

Beatty, Patricia. *How Many Miles to Sundown*. New York: William Morrow and Company, 1974. Grades 4 and up.

Three young people encounter bandits, Indians, and wild animals as they travel through the southwest looking for Nate's father and a town named Sundown.

_____. *Red Rocks over the River*. New York: William Morrow and Company, 1973. Grades 5 and up.

In 1881, two children come to Fort Yuma with their father. Their half-Indian housekeeper urges Dorcas, one of the children, to visit the Arizona Territorial Prison with her, and they write letters for the prisoners.

Gates, Doris. *Blue Willow*. New York: Viking Press, 1940. Grades 4 and up.

The daughter of a migrant worker, Janey yearns for permanence, yet must sell her willow plate to pay the rent. Having a home finally becomes a reality for the family.

Hausman, Sid. *Turtle Dream*. Santa Fe, N.M.: Mariposa Publishing, 1989. Grades 3 and up.

Hausman has collected these stories from his Native American friends in the Southwest. They include tales from the Hopi, Navaho, Pueblo, and Havasupai people.

Krumgold, Joseph. *...And Now Miguel*. Illustrated by Jean Charlot. New York: Thomas Y. Crowell, 1953. Grades 5 and up.

This is the true story of Miguel Chavez, a middle child in a family that raises sheep near Taos, New Mexico. Miguel yearns to be with the men who go to the Sangre de Cristo Mountains and faces a great adventure when he is allowed to pursue his dream.

O'Dell, Scott. *Carlota*. Boston: Houghton Mifflin Company, 1977. Grades 4 and up.

Carlota believes she is strong and unflinching until she wounds a young soldier in the Battle of San Pasqual in the 1840s.

Sebestyen, Ouida. *Words by Heart*. Boston: Little, Brown and Company, Inc., 1968. Grades 5 and up.

Lena's family was the only black family in a small Southwestern town. She yearns to gain her father's approval and to find a better life.

11
The West

Western states:
- Alaska
- California
- Colorado
- Hawaii
- Idaho
- Montana
- Nevada
- Oregon
- Utah
- Washington
- Wyoming

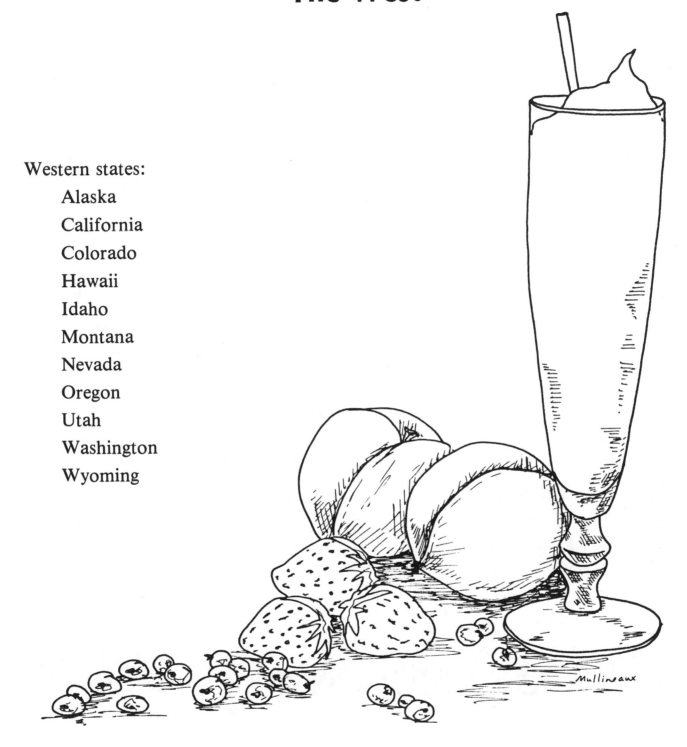

Chapter Eleven
Word List

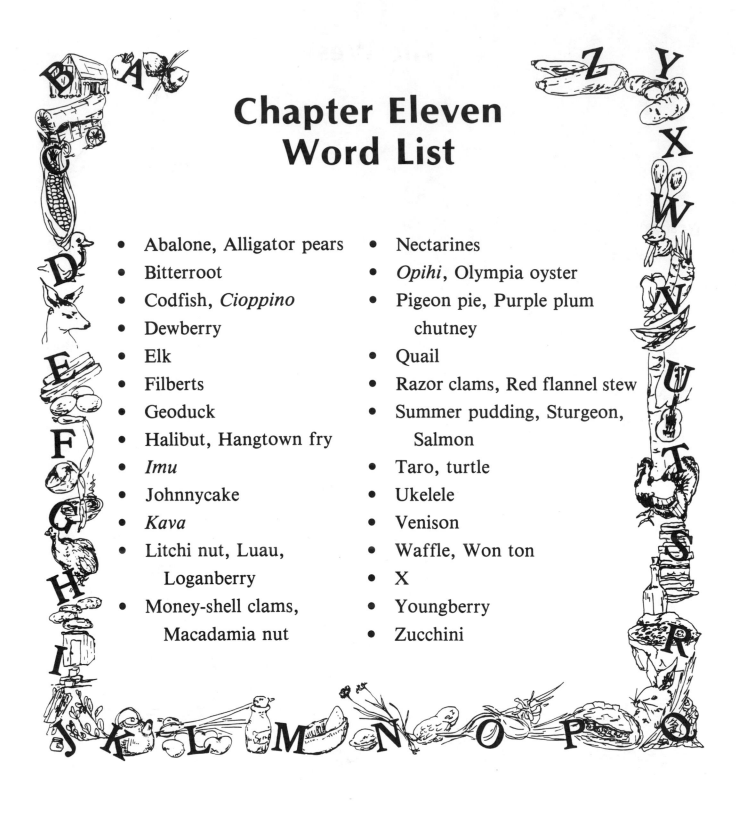

- Abalone, Alligator pears
- Bitterroot
- Codfish, *Cioppino*
- Dewberry
- Elk
- Filberts
- Geoduck
- Halibut, Hangtown fry
- *Imu*
- Johnnycake
- *Kava*
- Litchi nut, Luau, Loganberry
- Money-shell clams, Macadamia nut
- Nectarines
- *Opihi*, Olympia oyster
- Pigeon pie, Purple plum chutney
- Quail
- Razor clams, Red flannel stew
- Summer pudding, Sturgeon, Salmon
- Taro, turtle
- Ukelele
- Venison
- Waffle, Won ton
- X
- Youngberry
- Zucchini

WESTERN STEAK AND EGGS

Ingredients

2 6-ounce rib steaks, bone cut out
1½ cups coarse salt
Water
2 tablespoons oil

1½ tablespoons butter
4 eggs
Butter

Steps

1. Put 2 large frying pans on the stove.
2. Heat 1 pan to medium-high.
3. Mix salt with enough water to make a thick paste.
4. Spread paste on one side of the steaks. Put them paste side down in the hot frying pan.
5. Spread the other side of the steaks with the rest of the paste.
6. Cook steaks on both sides until crusty and done.
7. When steaks are almost finished frying, heat other pan on medium-low heat and melt the butter.
8. Fry eggs lightly as you like to eat them.
9. Remove steaks from pan. Scrape off all the salt coating.
10. Spread the top of steaks with butter. Serve immediately with eggs.

Serves 2.

Library Link 1: What method was used to preserve eggs in the 1800s?

DENVER OMELET

Ingredients

5 eggs
⅓ cup whole milk
½ teaspoon salt
1/8 teaspoon paprika
¼ teaspoon pepper
2 tablespoons butter

½ cup chopped green pepper
¼ cup chopped onion
⅔ cup chopped ham
1 cup grated cheese
    (Monterey Jack or cheddar)

Steps

1. Beat eggs with milk in a large mixing bowl.
2. Add salt, paprika, and pepper. Stir well.
3. In a large frying pan melt 1 tablespoon butter over medium heat. Add green pepper, onion, and ham. Cook for 5 minutes.
4. Put 1 tablespoon butter in omelet pan. Heat over medium-low heat.
5. Pour egg mixture into omelet pan. Lift edges with a pancake turner and tilt pan to let uncooked egg run underneath.
6. When egg is almost cooked through, sprinkle green pepper, onion, and ham mixture over half of egg mixture. Sprinkle with cheese.
7. Fold other half over and serve hot.

Serves 4.

Library Link 2: What are some proverbs or sayings that mention eggs?

PECAN WAFFLES

Ingredients
1 cup pecan halves
2 cups flour
½ teaspoon salt
2½ teaspoons baking powder
½ teaspoon baking soda
2 teaspoons sugar
4 eggs, separated
1 cup milk
1 cup sour milk*
4 tablespoons melted butter
1 cup finely chopped pecans
¼ teaspoon cream of tartar
Butter
Syrup, warmed

Steps
1. Heat oven to 325 degrees.
2. Put pecan halves on a cookie sheet.
3. Bake pecans until browned (15 to 20 minutes), stirring several times.
4. Remove from oven and set aside.
5. Put flour, salt, baking powder, baking soda, and sugar in a large mixing bowl.
6. Beat egg yolks well.
7. Stir egg yolks, milk, sour milk, melted butter, and chopped pecans into flour mixture.
8. Put egg whites in a medium glass or metal bowl. Add cream of tartar. Beat eggs with an electric mixer until stiff.
9. Carefully fold egg whites into flour mixture.
10. Cook waffles in waffle iron until browned.
11. Serve with baked pecan halves on top and butter and syrup on the side.

*To make sour milk, add 1 tablespoon of vinegar or lemon juice to milk and let sit for 10 minutes to curdle.

Serves 4.

Library Link 3:   What is the source and meaning of the word *waffle*?

CALIFORNIA DATE WALNUT BREAD

Ingredients
1½ cups pitted dates
1 cup sugar
1 cup water
½ cup shortening
2 eggs, beaten
2 cups flour
1½ teaspoons baking soda
½ teaspoon salt
¾ cup walnuts
2 teaspoons vanilla
Butter or cream cheese

Steps
1. Cut dates into small pieces.
2. Put dates and sugar in a large mixing bowl.
3. Put water in a medium saucepan and bring to a boil.
4. Add shortening to water and continue boiling water until shortening is melted. Remove from heat.
5. Pour water and shortening over dates and sugar. Stir well until sugar is dissolved.
6. Add eggs, beating well.
7. Add flour, baking soda, and salt. Mix in well.
8. Stir in walnuts and vanilla.
9. Put batter in a greased 9-by-5-inch loaf pan.
10. Bake at 325 degrees for 1 hour or until a toothpick inserted in the center comes out clean.
11. To serve, cut into thin slices. Top with butter or cream cheese.

Makes 1 loaf.

Library Link 4: A popular California drink is a date milkshake. How is it prepared?

FRUIT SOUP

Ingredients

1 pound raisins
½ pound pitted prunes
½ pound currants
½ pound raspberries
6 apples, peeled, cored, and quartered

Juice of ½ lemon
Sugar
3 cinnamon sticks
2 tablespoons cornstarch
Water

Steps

1. Put raisins, prunes, currants, raspberries, apples, and lemon juice in a large saucepan.
2. Cover with water and simmer for 2½ to 3 hours or until apples are very soft.
3. Add sugar to taste. Stir well.
4. Add cinnamon sticks.
5. Mix cornstarch with ¼ cup water in a small bowl.
6. Stir slowly into simmering fruit mixture.
7. Cook 5 more minutes.
8. Remove cinnamon sticks.
9. Serve hot or cold as a first course or as a dessert.

Serves 4 to 6.

Library Link 5: What are muscats?

COBB SALAD

Ingredients

½ head iceberg lettuce
6 leaves romaine lettuce
2 stalks celery, chopped
1 avocado, chopped
1 large tomato, chopped
1 cooked boneless chicken breast, chopped
2 hard boiled eggs, chopped
French, bleu cheese, or other salad dressing
2 ounces bleu cheese, crumbled
8 slices well done bacon, crumbled

Steps

1. Cut iceberg and romaine lettuce into bite-sized pieces. Put in large salad bowl.
2. Add celery, avocado, tomato, chicken, and eggs. Stir together.
3. Add dressing. Mix well.
4. Crumble cheese and bacon on top.

Serves 2 to 3.

Library Link 6: Who were the Delmonico brothers? What effect did they have on the eating habits of Americans?

SALMON LOAF

Ingredients

1 large can salmon
1 egg, beaten
½ cup evaporated milk
¾ cup soft bread crumbs
½ teaspoon salt
¼ teaspoon paprika
¼ teaspoon pepper

1 tablespoon lemon juice
2 teaspoons Worcestershire sauce
1 tablespoon melted butter
3 tablespoons chopped parsley
2 tablespoons chopped onion
¼ cup chopped olives

Steps

1. Drain and flake salmon. Put it in a large bowl.
2. Add egg and milk to salmon. Stir lightly.
3. Add rest of ingredients. Mix well.
4. Place mixture in a greased loaf pan.
5. Bake at 400 degrees for 25 to 30 minutes or until cooked through.
6. May be served with a cheese or Hollandaise sauce.

Serves 4.

Library Link 7: What river in the Northwest is known for its abundance of salmon?

CRAB LOUIS

Ingredients

1 cup mayonnaise
¼ cup heavy cream
¼ cup chili sauce
1 teaspoon Worcestershire sauce
¼ cup green pepper, chopped
¼ cup onion, chopped
2 tablespoons lemon juice

Salt and pepper to taste
Lettuce leaves
1 cup shredded lettuce
2½ cups cooked crab meat
    (Dungeness or Alaskan King)
2 hard boiled eggs
Chopped parsley

Steps

1. In a large mixing bowl stir together mayonnaise, cream, chili sauce, Worcestershire sauce, green pepper, onion, lemon juice, salt and pepper. Mix well into a smooth sauce.
2. Place lettuce leaves around the inside of salad bowls and add shredded lettuce.
3. Place cooked crab meat over shredded lettuce.
4. Pour sauce over crab meat.
5. Slice hard boiled eggs and place on top of sauce.
6. Sprinkle with parsley.

Serves 4.

Library Link 8: What area in the West boasts the greatest number of Dungeness crabs? What geological features foster this type of crab?

FRESH COLORADO TROUT

Ingredients
½ pound bacon
1 onion, sliced thin
⅔ cup yellow cornmeal
½ cup flour
1 tablespoon salt
1 teaspoon pepper
2 freshly caught trout, cleaned

Steps
1. In a large frying pan, fry bacon over medium-high heat.
2. Remove bacon from pan.
3. Put onion in a pan and fry in grease until soft.
4. Remove onion from pan.
5. Mix cornmeal, flour, salt, and pepper in a medium bowl.
6. Coat fish well with cornmeal mixture.
7. Fry fish in hot bacon grease over medium heat until browned on both sides.
8. Serve with bacon and onions sprinkled on top.

Serves 2.

Library Link 9:   What is a candlefish?

CIOPPINO

Ingredients

Sauce

2 tablespoons oil
4 tablespoons butter
1 small onion
3 sticks celery, chopped
1 carrot, chopped
½ green pepper, chopped
1 28-ounce can crushed tomatoes
1 tablespoon tomato paste
3½ cups water
3 teaspoons salt
½ teaspoon pepper
½ teaspoon thyme
4 bay leaves

2 pounds assorted seafood
(halibut, cod, scallops, etc.)
1 pound medium shrimp, shelled
and deveined
8 ounces crabmeat
2 tablespoons flour
2 tablespoons oil
4 tablespoons butter
1 teaspoon chopped garlic
½ cup water
½ cup chicken broth
1 dozen cherrystone clams
4 teaspoons chopped parsley

Steps

1. Put oil and butter in a large saucepan over medium-low heat.
2. Cook onion in oil and butter until soft.
3. Add celery, carrot, and pepper. Cook 5 minutes.
4. Add tomatoes, tomato paste, water, salt, pepper, thyme, and bay leaves. Cover.
5. Simmer 2 hours, stirring frequently.
6. Remove bay leaves.
7. Cut seafood into bite-sized pieces.
8. Dust assorted seafood, shrimp, and crabmeat with 2 tablespoons flour.
9. Put oil and butter in a large saucepan over medium-high heat.
10. Cook garlic in the oil and butter for 1 minute. Remove garlic from pan.
11. Add assorted seafood, shrimp, and crabmeat to heated oil and butter.
12. Cook over medium-high heat for 2 minutes until seafood is browned.
13. Add water and broth. Cook for 2 minutes.
14. Add tomato sauce to seafood. Cook for 5 minutes over low heat.
15. Steam clams. Discard clams that do not open.
16. Place clams on top. Sprinkle with parsley. Serve.

Serves 6.

Library Link 10: What does cioppino mean and where did it originate?

FILBERT CRESCENTS

Ingredients
1 cup confectioner's sugar
1 cup butter, softened
2 teaspoons vanilla
¼ teaspoon nutmeg
1 cup ground filberts
2½ cups flour
Confectioner's sugar for coating finished cookies

Steps
1. Sift confectioner's sugar.
2. Cream butter in a large bowl.
3. Gradually add sugar to butter. Mix well.
4. Stir in vanilla, nutmeg, and filberts.
5. Stir in 1½ cups flour.
6. Work in the other cup of flour with hands.
7. Roll the dough in waxed paper. Chill 1 hour.
8. Remove dough from refrigerator.
9. Roll or shape dough into crescent shapes.
10. Put cookies on a greased cookie sheet.
11. Bake at 350 degrees 10 to 12 minutes or until lightly browned.
12. Remove from oven.
13. Dip cookies in confectioner's sugar while still hot.

Makes 4 to 5 dozen.

Library Link 11:   What nut is most similar to the filbert?

CALIFORNIA SMOOTHIE

Ingredients
4 bananas
½ cup pitted dates
1 cup honey
2 cups crushed ice

2 cups strawberries
2 tablespoons bee pollen, optional
4 cups fruit juice

Steps

Note: Make ¼ of the recipe at a time in the blender.

1. Put banana, strawberries, and dates in the blender.
2. Mix on medium until smooth.
3. Add bee pollen and honey. Blend in.
4. Add juice and ice. Mix at high speed until well blended.
5. Serve immediately.

Makes 4 servings.

Library Link 12:   What causes variations in the taste of honey?

BIBLIOGRAPHY—THE WEST

Nonfiction

Canary, Martha. *Life and Adventures of Calamity Jane*. Wheatland, Wyo.: Triple R, 1970. Grades 4 and up.
Calamity Jane's life included roles as a teamster, Pony Express rider, hunter, rancher, nurse, wife, and mother.

Cleveland, Libra Jan. *Pacific Shores: The Pacific States*. Illustrated by Tom Dunnington. Chicago: Childrens Press, 1962. Grades 4 and up.
The history, exploration, people, parks, industries, and geographical features are described for the Pacific states: Alaska, California, Hawaii, Oregon and Washington.

Deloria, Vine. *Indians of the Pacific Northwest: From the Coming of the White Man to the Present Day*. Garden City, N.Y.: Doubleday and Company, Inc., 1977. Grades 6 and up.
Deloria covers the history of the Pacific Northwest Indians from the days when the Indians prospered in the area of Puget Sound to the time when the settlers' diseases had reduced their numbers and reservations were imposed upon them.

Ford, Douglas. *The Pacific Islanders*. New York: Chelsea House Publishers, 1989. Grades 5 and up.
Ford describes the histories and peoples of Hawaii, Polynesia, and Micronesia, and discusses their lives on the mainland. Many photographs provide insights into the people and their cultures.

Fordham, Derek. *Eskimos*. London: Macdonald Educational Ltd., 1979. Grades 3 and up.
This broad look at the life of the Eskimos is an excellent introduction for the beginning student researcher. The oversized photographs, drawings, and art work provide insights into the customs, home life, and challenges of the culture.

Friggens, Myriam. *Tales, Trails and Tommyknockers: Stories from Colorado's Past*. Illustrated by Gene Coulter. Boulder, Colo.: Johnson Publishing Company, 1979. Grades 3 and up.
Line drawings and photographs accompany this collection of stories about people from Colorado's past: Kit Carson, Chief Ouray, Molly Brown, and others.

Holder, Glenn. *Talking Totem Poles*. New York: Dodd, Mead and Company, 1973. Grades 4 and up.
The Northwest Coastal Indians erected totems to tell a story. Holder describes in text and black-and-white photographs the process of creating totems from tree selection to celebration at a potlatch.

Kirk, Ruth, and Richard D. Daugherty. *Hunters of the Whale: An Adventure in Northwest Coast Archaeology*. Photographs by Ruth and Louis Kirk. New York: William Morrow and Company, 1974. Grades 5 and up.
Ozette, a prehistoric Indian village, is excavated, and Daugherty assists with the documentation of the artifacts. Photographs of the process and intriguing text provide an instructive book.

Levine, Ellen. *If You Lived at the Time of the San Francisco Earthquake*. New York: Scholastic Book Services, 1987. Grades 2 and up.
From the circus animals who hovered close to the ground to the collapse of buildings, Levine tells the story of the 1906 earthquake in San Francisco.

Montgomery, Elizabeth Rider. *When a Ton of Gold Reached Seattle*. Illustrated by Raymond Burns. Champaign, Ill.: Garrard Publishing Company, 1968. Grades 3 and up.
In 1897 news of the gold strike in the Yukon Territory reached Seattle. Montgomery tells the story of Seattle's struggle to survive and prosper.

Place, Marian T. *Mount St. Helens: A Sleeping Volcano Awakes*. New York: Dodd, Mead and Company, 1981. Grades 5 and up.
The story of the eruption of Mount St. Helens is told with photographs and text about the event, its destruction, and aftermath.

Smith, J. H. Greg. *Eskimos: The Inuit of the Arctic*. Vero Beach, Fla.: Rourke Publications, Inc., 1987. Grades 3 and up.
Simple text and colorful photographs describe the lives of the ancient Inuit, the arrival of the settlers, and the transition into modern times.

Surge, Frank. *Western Lawmen*. Minneapolis, Minn.: Lerner Publications Company, 1969. Grades 3 and up.
Surge provides brief biographies of many western lawmen, including Wild Bill Hickok, Tom Smith, Bat Masterson, Wyatt Earp, and Judge Roy Bean.

_____. *Western Outlaws*. Minneapolis, Minn.: Lerner Publictions Company, 1969. Grades 3 and up.
Posters and photographs help illustrate the stories of Jesse James, Billy the Kid, Black Bart, Sam Bass, Belle Starr, the Daltons, and other notorious outlaws.

Williams, Terry T., and Ted Major. *The Secret Language of Snow*. Illustrated by Jennifer Dewey. New York: Pantheon Books, 1984. Grades 4 and up.
The Inuit people of Alaska rely on knowledge of snow conditions. Readers learn of their language and the descriptions of snow through the illustrations and text.

Wohlrabe, Raymond A. *The Pacific Northwest*. Cleveland, Ohio: The World Publishing Company, 1968. Grades 5 and up.
The history, exploration, settlement, industry, and recreation of Washington, Oregon, Idaho, and British Columbia are described.

Young, Bob, and Jan Young. *The Story of the Rocky Mountains*. New York: Hawthorn Books, Inc., 1969. Grades 4 and up.
This story begins with the birth of the mountains and their first inhabitants and continues to modern day.

Fiction

Arnston, Herbert E. *Frontier Boy: A Story of Oregon*. Illustrated by William Ferguson. New York: Ives Washburn, Inc., 1967. Grades 4 and up.
Living in the Northwest without the benefit of his father's guidance, Davy is challenged by the environment as well as the people of the era.

Beatty, Patricia. *The Coach That Never Came*. New York: William Morrow and Company, 1985. Grades 4 and up.

When Paul is sent to Colorado to spend the summer with his grandmother, he becomes involved in a 110-year-old mystery about a coach with $40,000 that disappeared.

_____. *Eight Mules from Monterey*. New York: William Morrow and Company, 1982. Grades 4 and up.

The Ashmore family has many adventures as they try to establish library outposts in the California wilderness.

_____. *Hail Columbia*. New York: William Morrow and Company, 1970. Grades 5 and up.

Columbia Baines arrives in Astoria in 1893 and disrupts the town with her beliefs in equality for women.

_____. *The Lady from Black Hawk*. New York: McGraw-Hill Book Company, 1967. Grades 3 and up.

Black Hawk, Colorado, is a boom town in 1884. Julie tries to cook and clean for her father and brothers, but decides it is time their father had a new wife.

_____. *Something to Shout About*. New York: William Morrow and Company, 1976. Grades 4 and up.

The women of Ottenberg, a gold mining town in the Montana territory, decide to raise money for a new school. Their fund-raising targets are the many saloons in the town.

Brown, Lisette G. *Tales of the Sea Foam*. Healdsburg, Calif.: Naturegraph Publishers, 1969. Grades 3 and up.

Seven stories tell of a white girl's experiences with Indians while she lived on the Northern California coast.

Corcoran, Barbara. *The Long Journey*. Illustrated by Charles Robinson. New York: Atheneum, 1970. Grades 4 and up.

Laurie has to travel by horse across 350 miles of Montana country to obtain medical help for her grandfather.

Fitzgerald, John D. *The Great Brain at the Academy*. Illustrated by Mercer Mayer. New York: The Dial Press, 1972. Grades 3 and up.

Tom and his great brain create trouble and fun at the Catholic Academy for boys in Salt Lake City. This is a sequel to *The Great Brain* (Dell, 1972).

George, Jean Craighead. *Julie of the Wolves*. New York: Harper and Row, 1972. Grades 5 and up.

At thirteen years of age, Julie runs away from an intolerable situation and becomes lost on the North Slope of Alaska. She is befriended by a tribe of wolves and survives.

Haynes, Nelma. *Panther Lick Creek*. Nashville, Tenn.: Abingdon Press, 1970. Grades 5 and up.

Two friends tangle with wild mustangs and a panther as they grow up in the new frontier of Texas.

Houston, James. *Eagle Mask: A West Coast Indian Tale*. New York: Harcourt Brace and World, 1966. Grades 4 and up.

Houston tells the story of Skemshan's coming of age as a prince of the Eagle clan in the Pacific Northwest.

_____. *Wolf Runs: A Caribou Eskimo Tale*. New York: Harcourt Brace Jovanovich, 1971. Grades 4 and up.

Punik, whose father had died, leaves his starving tribe to hunt for caribou. His chilling story demonstrates his courage.

Kent, Sherman. *A Boy and a Pig, but Mostly Horses*. Illustrated by Sam Savitt. New York: Dodd, Mead and Company, 1974. Grades 4 and up.
Kent uses his childhood experiences to tell the story of three boys who spend their summer on a Nevada ranch in the 1920s.

Lampman, Evelyn Sibley. *Go Up the Road*. Illustrated by Charles Robinson. New York: Atheneum, 1972. Grades 5 and up.
The Ruiz family is one of many migrant families who leave New Mexico to work on the Oregon fields. Yolanda's life is a series of struggles to become educated and find a better life.

_____. *The Potlatch Family*. New York: Atheneum, 1976. Grades 6 and up.
Plum Longor, a Pacific Coast Chinook Indian, feels others dislike her because of her dark skin and alcoholic father. The return of her brother results in the revival of their customs, bringing dignity to the Indians and their community.

_____. *Squaw Man's Son*. New York: Atheneum, 1978. Grades 5 and up.
Billy, who is half white and half Indian, leaves his home in Oregon and joins the Madocs, who eventually fight the whites. Billy is captured and released to his father. He realizes he doesn't fit in either world.

_____. *The Year of the Small Shadow*. New York: Harcourt Brace Jovanovich, 1971. Grades 5 and up.
When his father is sent to prison for stealing a horse, Small Shadow is sent to stay with the white lawyer who had helped his father. His experiences help others overcome their fears of the Indians.

Lord, Bette Bao. *The Year of the Boar and Jackie Robinson*. Illustrated by Marc Simont. New York: Harper and Row, 1984. Grades 3 and up.
Shirley Temple Wong's first year in San Francisco entertains readers with stories about language misunderstandings, school-time events, and the country's fascination with baseball.

O'Dell, Scott. *Island of the Blue Dolphins*. Boston: Houghton Mifflin Company, 1960. Grades 5 and up.
Karana is left with her brother on an island off the coast of California in the early 1800s. After her brother is killed by wild dogs she faces the challenges of the island alone.

_____. *Zia*. Boston: Houghton Mifflin Company, 1976. Grades 4 and up.
Zia embarks on a search for her aunt, moving to a Santa Barbara mission and challenging the sea in an attempt to rescue Karana. (Sequel to *Island of the Blue Dolphins*, above.)

Simonetta, Sam, and Linda Simonetta. *Trappers, Trains and Mining Claims*. Boulder, Colo.: Pruett Publishing Company, 1976. Grades 4 and up.
This is a collection of short stories about people and events in Colorado during the 1700s and 1800s.

Taylor, Theodore. *The Children's War*. Garden City, N.Y.: Doubleday and Company, Inc., 1971. Grades 5 and up.
Doug loved the Alaskan community where he could wander and hunt. But life changed when the Japanese bombed Pearl Harbor and the war crept closer to Doug.

Uchida, Yoshiko. *Journey Home*. Illustrated by Charles Robinson. New York: Atheneum, 1978. Grades 5 and up.
Yuki and her parents return to San Francisco from a World War II relocation center in Utah. This is a sequel to the story of their internment, *Journey to Topaz* (Berkeley, Calif., Creative Arts, 1985).

_____. *Samurai of Gold Hill*. Illustrated by Ati Forberg. New York: Charles Scribner's Sons, 1972. Grades 5 and up.
Uchida tells the story of a group of Japanese immigrants who come to California in 1869.

Yep, Laurence. *Dragonwings*. Illustrated by Nora S. Unwin. New York: E. P. Dutton, Inc., 1964. Grades 5 and up.
The life of a Chinese community in San Francisco in the early 1900s is described.

Bibliography: Books about Food

The following books were particularly helpful for historical and background information about foods of North America. Those that are written specifically for elementary children are noted. Other books are intended for adults but may be used by mature readers or for reference.

Anderson, Jean. *Recipes from America's Restored Villages*. Illustrated by Martin Silverman. Garden City, N.Y.: Doubleday and Company, Inc., 1975.
Anderson takes the reader on a culinary and historical tour of over forty restored villages across the United States. Recipes are included from past and present menus.

Giblin, James Cross. *From Hand to Mouth: Or, How We Invented Knives, Forks, Spoons, and Chopsticks and the Table Manners to Go with Them*. New York: Thomas Y. Crowell, 1987. Elementary.
Though not limited to North America, Giblin's account of the development of eating customs is an entertaining resource.

Herman, Judith, and Marguerite Shalett Herman. *The Cornucopia*. New York: Harper and Row, 1973.
The authors describe their book as "...a kitchen entertainment and cookbook containing good reading and good cookery from more than 500 years of recipes, food lore, etc., as conceived and expounded by the great chefs and gourmets of the old and new worlds between the years 1390 and 1899."

Perl, Lila. *Hunter's Stew and Hangtown Fry: What Pioneer America Ate and Why*. Illustrated by Richard Cuffari. New York: Seabury Press, 1977. Elementary.
Perl explores the role of food throughout the westward movement. She includes the adaptations of food made necessary by the conditions as well as the contributions of immigrant groups. Selected recipes are included. This is suitable for intermediate students to read.

_____. *Red-flannel Hash and Shoo-fly Pie*. Illustrated by Eric Carle. Cleveland, Ohio: The World Publishing Company, 1965. Intermediate.
Perl provides a regional and historical exploration of food in America. This is an excellent resource book for student researchers.

_____. *Slumps, Grunts, and Snickerdoodles: What Colonial America Ate and Why*. Illustrated by Richard Cuffari. Boston: Houghton Mifflin Company, 1975. Elementary.
The importance of food in colonial times is thoroughly discussed by Perl. The key recipes of the period are included. This is suitable for intermediate students to read.

Root, Waverly, and Richard de Rochemont. *Eating in America: A History*. New York: William Morrow and Company, 1976.
This five hundred-page history should be the first source for anyone interested in learning about food in America. The authors have provided extensive information on virtually every aspect of the subject. No recipes are included.

Tannahill, Reay. *Food in History*. New York: Stein and Day, 1973.
This extensive book provides background information on food throughout the world from prehistoric days to the present. Though not specific to North America, the role of food in the New World is included. No recipes are included.

Visser, Margaret. *Much Depends on Dinner: The Extraordinary History and Mythology, Allure and Obsessions, Perils and Taboos of an Ordinary Meal*. New York: Grove Press, 1986.
Visser uses an ordinary meal of corn, butter, chicken, rice, salad with lemon juice and oil, and ice cream to delve into the history, issues, and practices surrounding each item.

Williams, Barbara. *Cornzapoppin'! Popcorn Recipes and Party Ideas for All Occasions*. Photographs by Royce L. Bair. New York: Holt, Rinehart and Winston, 1976.
Though primarily recipes and projects using popcorn, Williams provides a brief, fascinating history of popcorn in America.

OTHER

For a catalog of maple products, write to:

Polly's Pancake Parlor
Hildex Farm
Sugar Hill, NH 03585

Appendix A
Answers to Library Links

CHAPTER ONE: THE AMERICAN INDIANS

1. Pawcohiccora is the Virginian Indian name for hickory nut.
2. Peanut butter, peanut oil, soap, face powder, shampoo, feed for cattle and pigs. The shells are used for plastics, wallboard, linoleum, and polishes.
3. Nuts were ground with stones.
4. Pemmican was carried in packets of animal skin.
5. Beans were found in objects dating from 5000 B.C. excavated in Mexican caves.
6. Corn began as a wild grass.
7. Squash was baked whole in ashes or embers of a dying fire.
8. Diggings in Mexico City revealed evidence of corn grains 60,000 to 80,000 years old.
9. Wild rice, which was not truly rice, was found near the Great Lakes. It grew in water and was called Indian rice or water oats by the settlers.
10. Sukquttahash, msakwitash, m'sick-quotash are examples of American Indian spellings of succotash.
11. Answers will vary. Many tribes had well defined table manners, and included prayer before meal and formal thanks at the end of a meal. In some tribes the husband waited on the guests. Plains Indians brought their own dishes with them and took them home for washing.
12. Answers will vary. The American Indians were sophisticated farmers. They developed many varieties of beans and corn. They planted efficiently, knowing what vegetables to plant together to maximize the use of the soil without depleting it.
13. The settlers brought slips of apple trees to New England and found that they grew better in America than in England.
14. American Indians would put a whole ear on a stick and hold it over the fire. They would also throw loose kernels into the fire, and when the kernels burst they would pop out of the fire. They would also heat a clay pot by pouring hot sand into it and put it over the fire. When it was hot they would remove the pot, pour the popcorn into the hot sand and stir it with a stick. The popcorn would pop to the top for eating.

CHAPTER TWO: THE COLONIAL PERIOD

1. Oats are a cereal grass. They were used for food and to feed horses. Oats were important as horse feed because horses allowed the colonists to hunt and travel.
2. The American Indian word for corn is *maize*. Corn is a cereal plant and was introduced to the Pilgrims by the Indians. The climate in England was not conducive to the growth of corn.
3. Pilgrims dried the corn before grinding it into a coarse powder with a stone or wooden mortar and pestle. They used cornmeal because it was more plentiful.

4. Life was basic. Their diet was a mix of English and Indian foods. The colonists primarily ate game birds, pork, and chicken for meat. They ate corn flour rather than wheat flour. They had little sugar or molasses for many years. They had to rely on what was readily available to them in America.

5. The Pilgrims used dark beers and ales as sweeteners.

6. Answers will vary.

7. The bean plant is a legume. Other legumes are peanuts and coffee beans. Legumes could be dried for later use and endured long storage periods.

8. Squash is harvested primarily in late summer and fall. The success of the harvest determined the amount of food the colonists would have during the next year.

9. Clam chowder is well known. Chowders are popular on the coasts because of the availability of clams and fish.

10. The Pilgrims would have to dry the corn and beans for winter use. They would then have to soak them in water before making succotash.

11. The Pilgrims learned about pumpkins from the Indians. Some examples of literature featuring pumpkins are "Peter, Peter, pumpkin eater"; *The Vanishing Pumpkin* by Tomie DePaola; and various Halloween stories.

12. A quill is a feather from the large tail of a bird, such as a turkey. A section of the end was sliced off, sliced again to shape it, and then split.

13. Early Americans used cut-up linen rags that were washed and boiled with lye until the cloth had disintegrated. The lye was washed away and the remaining mass was reduced to pulp. A mold was dipped into the mass. For a more detailed explanation, refer to *Colonial Living* by Edwin Tunis (see Chapter 2 bibliography). For paper-making directions for children, see *Paper by Kids* by Arnold E. Grummer (Minneapolis, Minn.: Dillon Press, 1980).

14. Answers will vary.

15. Bees secrete wax, used for candles. Sheep provided tallow. Good candles could be made from the wax of bayberries.

16. Molds were made by blacksmiths. Most candles were dipped because molds were unavailable until artisans were able to set up shop. Molds were made of tin or sometimes pewter. Eventually traveling chandlers, or candlemakers, brought large molds to a house and made up a family's stock.

17. Answers will vary.

CHAPTER THREE: REVOLUTIONARY WAR

1. "Sap's rising" means that the sap is moving through the trees. Actually the sap moves every direction, not just up.

2. Most spices were imported, and many new lands were discovered in the quest of finding spices. Spices were used in meat dishes to disguise the taste of the often-spoiled meat.

3. Sweet potatoes are grown on a climbing vine in warmer climates than white potatoes, which grow underground. They were used because of their availability and appealing taste.

4. They cooked over open fires in black pots or in crude ovens. Sometimes a cake might be burned on one end and raw on the other end. They might try to bake by putting hot stones on top of a covered pot to distribute the heat more evenly.

5. Answers will vary. A pudding stone is a conglomerate.

6. Pies for company were kept in a chest. The word chess is thought to be a form of *chest*, indicating that the pie was kept in a chest until needed.

7. A pound cake was made by actually weighing items. Eggs were smaller and the number needed for a cake would vary depending on size. Sugar had to be pounded out from a loaf or cone. Flour was coarse and very heavy.

   The tea parties were "tealess" to protest the British tax on tea.

8. "Little Miss Muffet." The first cows were brought in the early 1600s. Some reports state that they were brought to the Jamestown colony in 1611. Others state that they arrived in 1624.
9. Strawberries, blueberries, blackberries, raspberries, elderberries, and currants.
10. John Chapman was born in Massachusetts in 1774. He began planting seeds in 1799 and traveled for forty years, planting and tending his trees.

CHAPTER FOUR: WESTWARD EXPANSION

1. Leather Britches Beans were made with green beans or pole beans that were dried in the sun for several days. When dried, they were soaked in cold water overnight and then cooked with salt pork or fatback till soft.
2. Prospectors were called sourdoughs because they often carried a pot with a pinch of sourdough in it. Their staples were beans, pork, and sourdough or baking soda biscuits.
3. Sourdough originated in Egypt, over 6000 years ago. It was the only way of leavening bread.
4. Modern technology made yeast, baking soda, and baking powder readily available, and sourdough was no longer needed to leaven bread.
5. Baking soda was called saleratus.
6. Corn was removed from the cob and dried in the sun.
7. *Frijoles* is the Mexican name for beans. The word pinto means spotted.
8. Answers will vary.
9. Tomatoes originated in South America and were taken to Europe, where they were used as an ornamental plant for two hundred years. They were brought back to America in the early 1800s. Many people thought tomatoes were poisonous or caused cancer.
10. Cranberries grow in cool, wet, sandy areas called bogs. Bogs are found in the Northeast and Northwest, near the coasts.

CHAPTER FIVE: THE CIVIL WAR

1. Gail Borden worked hard at preserving foods, wanting to provide food that would travel. His factory was comandeered by the government to produce condensed milk for the soldiers, who became proponents of the product, ensuring its continued use after the war.
2. Holes were added to dough nuts at the turn of the century (1900).
3. Potatoes came to Spain from Peru and were brought to Virginia by the colonists.
4. Weevils are a slim brown bug, 1/8 inch in length. They would bore through hardtack.
5. The Homestead Act provided virtually free, formerly untilled land to would-be farmers. The abundance of food that subsequently became available benefitted both the North and Europe.
6. In brief, the North had available an abundance of land, made available and fruitful through the Homestead Act. The soil of the South was exhausted through the planting of cotton and tobacco. When the plantations were converted to food production, the harvests were disappointing.
7. Sherman devastated the food supplies and crops as he swept through the South. When the war was ended, one of the first acts of the government was to rush food to the Confederate troops.
8. Ginger was imported from Jamaica, India, and the African countries of Sierra Leone and Nigeria.
9. Approximately three shillings.
10. The cacao bean was dried and roasted over a fire. It was pounded into a powder. Sometimes sugar or other spices were added.
11. Other coffee substitutes were parched corn, peanuts, chicory, sweet potatoes, and rye.

CHAPTER SIX: THE NORTHEAST

1. The bilberry is an English shrub that bears fruit that is very similar to blueberries. The colonists often confused them. The species is *Vaccinium*.
2. Oliver Evans began producing bolted flour in his watermill in the 1780s, and the use of flour became common by the 1830s.
3. The fat of pigs would be rendered for lard that was used for frying and for soap.
4. Bivalved means the two shells are hinged together.
5. The cherrystone clam is larger.
6. Coon oysters are mollusks about 2 inches long. They are so small that they are difficult to obtain in large quantities. They are favored by raccoons, thus the name of coon oysters.
7. Hash means something that is a jumble. It also means something that has been worked over.
8. Types of clam include: pompano or coquina, littleneck, cherrystone, butter, razor, geoduck, Ipswich.
9. The edible part of the beet that is included in this recipe is the root. The leaves can be served in a salad.
10. Cranberries were first called crane berries because the shape of the blossom was like the head of a crane. It was shortened to cranberries later.
11. To "dowdy" means to cut up, as the crust is cut up after the first round of baking. A pandowdy has come to be known as a deep-dish pudding or pie made of apples.
12. The pumpkin plants helped keep down the weeds.

CHAPTER SEVEN: THE MID-ATLANTIC STATES

1. In addition to rye, corn, wheat, and buckwheat are grown in Pennsylvania.
2. The first commercial pretzel bakeries were established in the 1860s.
3. Matzoh balls are eaten by Jews during the feast of Passover.
4. Maryland wraps around Chesapeake Bay, providing an abundance of shoreline and access to oyster beds.
5. Soft-shell crabs have recently shed their shells and have not grown a larger shell yet.
6. Holstein cows are used now because they produce about twice as much milk.
7. The name may have come from the Dutch word *snekrad*, meaning snail wheel, a wheel in clockworks. Another possible source is the German word *schnecke*, meaning snail and referring to the pinwheel shape.
8. The sweet, sticky molasses at the top of the pie attracted flies and they had to be shooed away.
9. Zwieback is a kind of rusk or finger-shaped dry or toasted cake.
10. Henry Hudson.
11. Hex signs ward off evil spirits.
12. Dolly Madison (1809).

CHAPTER EIGHT: THE SOUTHEAST

1. Grits were usually served with ham at breakfast.
2. Grits come from hominy that is ground into coarse meal.
3. A popular theory, though unproven, is that hush puppies got their name when a Southern black cook threw a bit of one to a barking puppy, calling, "Hush, puppy." See Barbara Mitchell's *Hush Puppies* (chapter eight bibliography).
4. Butter, fat, or lard are used to make pastry short (tender and flaky).
5. Louisiana.

6. Stack cakes were wedding cakes. Guests would bring layers and stack them. It was said that the taller the finished stack the more popular the bride.
7. The Zuni made dumplings of blue cornmeal, called blue marbles.
8. King Henry VIII.
9. Americans eat about 250,000 tons of peanut butter each year.
10. To make candied fruit, boil ¾ cup sugar and ¼ cup water to soft-ball stage (236 degrees). Dip fruit in the syrup and dry on baking sheet.
11. Pralines.

CHAPTER NINE: THE MIDWEST AND PRAIRIES

1. True cinnamon is from the bark of a tree from Sri Lanka and the Malabar Coast. A similar bark from Vietnam is used for cassia cinnamon.
2. When a girl drops a chunk of bread into the fondue, the men may kiss her.
3. The refrigerated railroad car allowed the transportation of cut meat without spoilage.
4. Pasties originally came from Cornwall.
5. T. A. Dorgan, a cartoonist, drew a frankfurter with thick legs and a head which became known as a hot dog.
6. Eel, elver, and shad are sea or fresh water fish, depending on their age or season.
7. Angel food cake originated in St. Louis, Missouri.
8. The early settlers called this dessert strawberry bread.
9. Johnny Appleseed obtained his seeds from cider presses in western Pennsylvania.
10. Spritz is a German word and means "to squirt."

CHAPTER TEN: THE SOUTHWEST

1. Tortillas are made from corn and wheat.
2. Pueblos, Hopis, Zunis, Comanches, Kiowas, Apaches, and Navahos lived in the Southwest.
3. Types of bean include broad, black, turtle, cranberry, scarlet runner, red, kidney, black-eyed peas or beans, chick-peas or garbanzos, soy, flageolets, adzuki, pinto, and cowpeas or Mexican frijoles.
4. Chili con carne is believed to have been created in San Antonio, Texas, in the late 1800s.
5. Tamales are wrapped in cornhusks.
6. Applejack is distilled cider.
7. Sometimes called "sopa" in New Mexico, the Spanish called it "spotted dog" because of the raisins in it.
8. The Sioux Indians enjoyed *Wo-Japi*.
9. *Biscochitos* are a popular Christmas cookie in New Mexico.
10. *Barbecue* came from the Spanish word *barbacoa*, meaning a framework of sticks.
11. *Pinole* is a Mexican Indian beverage.

CHAPTER ELEVEN: THE WEST

1. Eggs were preserved in the 1800s by immersing them in a water-and-lime solution or by greasing them with melted mutton fat and storing them in a box of bran.
2. Answers will vary. Examples follow: "A kiss without a moustache is like an egg without salt" (old Spanish saying). "No wonder, Child, we prize the Hen, Whose Egg is mightier than the Pen" (Oliver Herford). "Don't put all your eggs in one basket."
3. Waffle is a German word that means "weave" or "honeycomb."

4. Blend ¾ cup chopped dates and ½ cup milk until smooth in a blender. Add a pint of ice cream and ½ cup milk. Blend and serve.
5. Muscats are white raisins.
6. The Delmonico brothers opened a restaurant in New York City. They popularized salads by introducing endive, eggplant, and other unusual foods.
7. The Columbia River, between Oregon and Washington, has an abundance of salmon.
8. Puget Sound, Washington, offers more than two hundred miles of coast that has a mild climate conducive to Dungeness crab.
9. A candlefish is an oily fish that, when dried, can be lit and burned as a candle.
10. Cioppino originated on the San Francisco wharves and means to "chip in" to the stew kettle.
11. The hazelnut is similar to the filbert.
12. The taste of honey is affected by the soil, climate, and nearby flowers, plants, trees, and bushes visited by the bees.

Appendix B
Measurements

HOW TO MEASURE ACCURATELY

Flour
Dip measuring cup into flour. Level off extra with a knife.

Sugar (granulated or confectioner's)
Spoon into a measuring cup. Level off with a knife.

Brown sugar
Pack brown sugar into a measuring cup. It should hold its shape when turned out of the cup.

Shortening
Use a spatula or scraper to pack it into a measuring cup. Level off with a knife.

Liquids
Pour into cup. A glass liquid measuring cup allows extra room at the top, preventing spilling.

Molasses and syrup "round" up, so pour slowly. Use a spatula or rubber scraper to scrape out cup.

Nuts, coconut, bread crumbs, cheese, etc.
Pack measuring cup lightly until full.

Spices, baking powder, salt, etc.
Stir. Fill measuring spoon and level off with a knife.

MEASURING EQUIVALENTS

Dash = less than 1/8 teaspoon

3 teaspoons = 1 tablespoon

4 tablespoons = ¼ cup

5⅓ tablespoons = ⅓ cup

8 tablespoons = ½ cup

10⅔ tablespoons = ⅔ cup

12 tablespoons = ¾ cup

16 tablespoons = 1 cup

1 cup = ½ pint

2 cups = 1 pint

2 pints (4 cups) = 1 quart

Butter or Margarine

4 sticks = 1 pound = 2 cups

1 stick = ¼ pound = ½ cup

½ stick = 1/8 pound = ¼ cup

1/8 stick = 1 tablespoon

Eggs

Whole Medium	Whites	Yolks
1 = ¼ cup	2 = ¼ cup	3 = ¼ cup
2 = ⅓ to ½ cup	3 = 3/8 cup	4 = ⅓ cup
3 = ½ to ⅔ cup	4 = ½ cup	5 = 3/8 cup
4 = ⅔ to 1 cup	5 = ⅔ cup	6 = ½ cup

Appendix C
Altitude Adjustments

Cakes:

At high elevations up to 3,000 feet:
Raise the baking temperature about 25 degrees.
Underbeat the eggs.

At elevations above 3,000 feet:
Raise the baking temperature about 25 degrees.
Reduce the double-acting baking powder or baking soda by 1/8 teaspoon for each teaspoon called for in
     the recipe.
Underbeat the eggs.

At 5,000 feet:
Raise the baking temperature about 25 degrees.
Reduce the double-acting baking powder or baking soda by ¼ teaspoon for each teaspoon called for in
     the recipe.
Underbeat the eggs.
Decrease sugar 1 to 2 tablespoons for each cup.
Increase liquid 2 to 3 tablespoons for each cup.

For all high altitudes:
Grease and flour all baking pans well. Cakes tend to stick.

WATER:

Boiling temperatures (Fahrenheit)

Sea level	212 degrees
2,000 feet	208 degrees
5,000 feet	203 degrees
7,500 feet	198 degrees

CANDY:

For each increase of 500 feet above sea level, cook candy syrups 1 degree lower than indicated in the recipes.

BREADS:

Reduce the baking soda or baking powder by one-fourth.

Glossary of Cooking Terms

Bake. To cook in an oven.

Beat. To mix with vigorous over-and-under motion with a spoon, whip, or beater.

Blend. To mix thoroughly.

Boil. To cook liquid until bubbles break on the surface.

Chill. To allow to become thoroughly cold, usually by placing in a refrigerator.

Chop. To cut in fine or coarse pieces with a knife.

Coat. To cover with thin film, such as with flour, crumbs, or sugar.

Cool. To allow to cool to room temperature.

Core. To remove the core of a fruit.

Cream. To work shortening and sugar against the side of a bowl with a spoon or to beat with a mixer until thoroughly blended and creamy.

Cut in. To mix fat into flour using a pastry blender, fork, or two knives.

Dice. To cut into small (about ¼-inch) cubes.

Fold in. To cut through the center of batter with a spoon, scraper, or spatula, bringing the spoon up close to the bowl, and cutting down through again, around the bowl, until blended.

Frost. To cover with icing.

Fry. To fry in a pan in shortening or oil.

Grate. To reduce to small particles by rubbing against a grater.

Grind. To cut or crush with a food or nut grinder.

Hull. To remove the stem or hull of a fruit.

Knead. To work dough by pressing, folding, and stretching with the hands.

Mash. To mix or crush to a soft form.

Mix. To combine ingredients by stirring.

Pare or peel. To remove the outside skin.

Pit. To remove pits or seeds from fruit.

Puree. To push fruit or vegetables through a sieve.

Rinse. To wash lightly, usually with water.

Roast. To cook by dry heat, usually in oven.

Roll. To place on a board and spread thin with a rolling pin.

Sauté. To cook or fry in a small amount of oil, shortening, or butter in a skillet.

Scald. To heat to temperature just below the boiling point until a skin forms on top.

Score. To cut narrow gashes partway through the outer surface.

Shred. To cut or tear into small slices or bits.

Shuck. To peel off the outer layer.

Sift. To pass through a sieve to remove lumps.

Simmer. To cook in liquid just below the boiling point.

Slice. To cut a thin, flat piece off.

Soak. To immerse in liquid.

Steam. To cook in steam that arises from a pan of boiling liquid.

Stir. To mix with a spoon.

Strain. To remove excess liquid, perhaps with a strainer or sieve.

Toss. To lightly mix ingredients.

Whip. To beat rapidly to incorporate air into the batter.

Index

About the Authors

Suzanne I. Barchers

Patricia Marden

Suzanne I. Barchers received her bachelor of science degree in elementary education from Eastern Illinois University, her master's degree in education in reading from Oregon State University and her doctor of education degree in curriculum and instruction from University of Colorado, Boulder.

Suzanne has been an educator and administrator in public and private schools for fifteen years. She is a contributing author to *Learning* magazine's "The Literature Center" and is the author of *Creating and Managing the Literate Classroom* and *Wise Women: Folk and Fairy Tales from around the World.* Suzanne has served as adjunct faculty for University of Colorado, Denver, and is a frequent speaker at regional and national conventions.

Suzanne currently resides in Arvada, Colorado, with her husband, Dan, and sons, Jeff and Josh. She was formerly Director of Education at the Denver Children's Museum and is now an Acquisitions Editor for Teacher Ideas Press, a division of Libraries Unlimited. She continues to write in the area of language arts.

Patricia Marden received her bachelor's degree in elementary education and master's degree in reading at the University of Delaware. She was a primary school teacher and administrator in Hockessin, Delaware, for ten years before moving to Colorado in 1982.

Patricia has received several grants and is involved in many professional groups that are investigating areas of alternative assessment, the writing process, literature-based reading, animals in the classroom, real-life mathematics using problem-solving approaches, cooperative grouping of students, and computer-aided learning.

Patricia currently resides in Aurora, Colorado, with her husband and daughter and is teaching in the Cherry Creek School District in Englewood. She enjoys using a teaching method that integrates all subject areas into a central theme. Cooking and children's literature are employed to teach a wide variety of skills and to motivate her children.